Library of
Davidson College

VERSIONS OF HEROISM IN MODERN AMERICAN DRAMA

Versions of Heroism in Modern American Drama

Redefinitions by Miller, Williams, O'Neill and Anderson

JULIE ADAM

St. Martin's Press New York

812.09
A194v

© Julie Adam 1991

All rights reserved. For information, write:
Scholarly and Reference Division,
St. Martin's Press, Inc., 175 Fifth Avenue,
New York, N.Y. 10010

First published in the United States of America in 1991

Printed in Hong Kong

ISBN 0-312-05779-2

Library of Congress Cataloging-in-Publication Data
Adam Julie, 1955-
Versions of heroism in modern American drama : redefinitions by Miller, O'Neill, and Anderson / Julie Adam.
p. cm.
Includes bibliographical references and index.
ISBN 0-312-05779-2
1. American drama (Tragedy)—History and criticism. 2. American drama—20th century—History and criticism. 3. Miller, Arthur, 1915- —criticism and interpretation. 4. O'Neill, Eugene, 1888-1953—Criticism and interpretation. 5. Anderson, Maxwell, 1888-1959—Criticism and interpretation. 6. Heroes in literature.
I. Title.
PS336.T7A3 1991
812'.05120905—dc20 90-48822
CIP

ACF-8124

92-9091

To my Parents

Contents

Acknowledgements

I wish to thank Frederick J. Marker, my former thesis supervisor, for his guidance and encouragement during the writing of the dissertation, a project out of which this book grew. My appreciation also goes to Alexander Leggatt for offering his advice about possible revisions. Last, but certainly not least, I wish to thank my parents, Jan Adam and Zuzana Adam, for providing various forms of support, emotional and otherwise; in particular, I am indebted to my mother for fostering in me an early interest in literature and to my father for not trying to steer me to a more practical career.

Introduction

I

This book is an exploration of redefinitions. It considers the various ways in which Arthur Miller, Tennessee Williams, Eugene O'Neill and Maxwell Anderson approach the issue of dramatic heroism and the related literary problem of modern tragedy. During my research of critical approaches to modern dramatic tragedy I became interested in the fascination tragedy has held for numerous playwrights, and in the fervour with which a number of practitioners of modern drama have insisted on being considered part of an uninterrupted tradition of tragedy. In spite of working within an American liberal democratic setting, with its optimistic tendencies and its glorification of individualism, these dramatists wish to emulate a dramatic form reflecting a philosophy of life and a view of the world totally alien to their own and to those of their culture and possibly, as some have suggested, no longer relevant for the modern age.

One critical cliché says that there can be no heroism in literary works because there are no instances of heroism in modern life. Anyone having the benefit of a lack of acquaintance with the literary world will know that such an estimate of the contemporary world and its inhabitants is nonsense. When critics and writers refer to the lack of heroism in the modern era frequently they are not only glorifying the past and measuring the present against a past that is occasionally a figment of their imagination but also, I suspect, more often than not referring not to life but to art. That is, the modern literary imagination is non-heroic – grounded in an essentially democratic, egalitarian philosophy – and yet often excessively preoccupied with questions of heroism.

Some playwrights' desire to belong to an exclusive club of 'classic' writers – for instance, practitioners of tragedy – is understandable in view of the overwhelming power of the popular, especially in the United States. The American interest in literary tragedy and heroism in the twentieth century has, I believe, to do with a passionately felt need to be part of an uninterrupted literary tradition and to see a direct, glorious line from the ancients – in the case of tragedy,

Aristotle and the Greek dramatists whose works he describes in the *Poetics* – to the moderns.

The playwrights examined here can be viewed as 'traditional' in the sense that Eliot, in his 'Tradition and the Individual Talent', defines the word in his discussion of the 'historical sense'. He states that

> . . . the historical sense involves a perception, not only of the pastness of the past, but of its presence; the historical sense compels a man to write not merely with his own generation in his bones, but with a feeling that the whole of the literature of Europe from Homer and within it the whole of the literature of his own country has a simultaneous existence and composes a simultaneous order. This historical sense, which is a sense of the timeless and of the temporal together, is what makes a writer traditional. And it is at the same time what makes a writer most acutely conscious of his place in time, of his contemporaneity. (4)

An American-turned-Englishman, Eliot consciously and deliberately sets out to place himself and his culture within 'the whole of . . . literature'. His insistence on the coexistence of past and present is indicative of both a historical sense and an awareness of a relative lack of historical dimension in his country of origin. Eliot discovers the obvious: that art does not exist in a vacuum; that there is no understanding of the present without an understanding of the past. What also emerges from his analysis, however, is an acute concern not only with the origins of the present in the past, and the dependence of the modern on the traditional, but also with the weighty presence of the past. Furthermore, although Eliot hints at a historical development, or a process, his controlling image in the discussion is the mosaic, the collage (as in 'The Wasteland') and his sense of the past is mythical rather than strictly political or even historical, in the usual contemporary sense of the word.

The four playwrights under examination use the past – both personal and social – in a similar manner, and this tells us something about their approach to heroism and tragedy. Although their dramas do not have the intellectual weight of Eliot's writings, and the 'history' they dramatize is often a private history, their analysis of the relationship between past and present – as revealed through such figures as Willy Loman, Blanche DuBois, James Tyrone, and others – partakes of an awareness, comparable to Eliot's, of the presence of the past. Miller's *After the Fall* best illustrates the problematic relationship of past to present, of political reality to private survival and ultimately of social and individual action to public and private guilt. The play is an apolitical and ahistorical dramatization of history; it is an entirely internalized view of the past – historical and political reality as stream-of-consciousness. As the title suggests, history is life after the Fall; history – in the most sinister guises of McCarthyite betrayals and of Nazi atrocities – here emblematizes knowledge, or more specifically, consciousness of evil, and thus must necessarily lead to guilt. Clearly, such an understanding of the past is moralized and mythical, rather than strictly political. In such diverse plays as Miller's *Death of a Salesman* and *After the Fall*, O'Neill's *Long Day's Journey into Night* and Williams' *A Streetcar Named Desire* the characters' attitudes to the past are ambivalent: the past is a place they must flee but also a haven from the present; it seems to be separate from the present and yet an inextricable part of it. On a private scale, in *Death of a Salesman*, the past is not merely where Willy came from, but rather exists simultaneously with the present. Interestingly enough, the past in these plays is a place rather than a time, and thus is not only recalled by the characters but also lived in. The transparent 'walls' of the set of *Death of a Salesman, A Streetcar Named Desire, The Glass Menagerie*, as well as other plays, facilitate the simultaneous dramatization of past and present. Repeatedly, various characters – for instance Willy Loman, Blanche DuBois, Mary Tyrone, Quentin – appear to be living in the present but in the course of the play discover that they are firmly – some more so than others – planted in the past and that their hold on the present is tenuous at best. This understanding of the past and consequent dramatic use of the past is very different from Ibsen's usage in such plays as *A Doll House, The Wild Duck* or Strindberg's in *Miss Julie*. As in Eliot's schema, the past is not simply a sequence of events leading up to the present and exerting an influence on it, but rather events occurring simultaneously with 'present' events and thus inevitably complicating them.

Miller's and Williams' approaches to tragedy depend on their attitudes to and treatment of the past in their plays. They, as well as O'Neill and Anderson, appropriate the tradition of tragedy; for them the tragic view of life is not a philosophy of a specific culture with its particular assumptions about existence clearly tied to a well-defined era, but rather a 'timeless' approach to life and art. They believe that tragedy dramatizes a way of looking at individual existence that must not disappear for it says something about 'man' that we moderns are not able to express. They use this ancient form – or rather their own version of it – to insist on the overwhelming presence of the past and mainly on the timelessness of their own writings. Even more importantly, however, the genre is used to comment on the present and to endow the modern with dignity through its association with the traditional. The literary tradition within which they believe they are working provides a backdrop, a context and a valorization. Heroism in the plays of Miller, Williams, O'Neill and Anderson is redefined to suit contemporary ideas and yet functions by reference to traditional ideas.

One might be justified in wondering why it is necessary to relate contemporary views of human dignity to those of the past and to make traditional terms apply to new standards of behavior and of dramatic representation in a modern socio-political context with very different power relationships. However, it is significant that playwrights and critics repeatedly gauge these concepts against classical and Renaissance norms. When Miller, in 'Tragedy and the Common Man' and in 'The Nature of Tragedy', tries to justify Willy's heroism, he measures the actions of the 'common man' against precepts of the past. He contends that criteria for heroism must necessarily undergo change; nevertheless, his discussion cannot escape the constant references to traditional concepts. As a consequence, although he redefines stature, nobility and suffering, he still considers them the marks of the heroic protagonist.

In studying these selected plays in terms of their explorations of heroism, I am looking at restatements of traditional concepts, often as a response to a possible break with tradition, and an amalgamation of disparate ideas, such as the union of sociological treatise and tragedy in *Death of a Salesman*, sexual melodrama and tragedy in *A Streetcar Named Desire*, or autobiography and tragedy in *Long Day's Journey into Night*.

Attempts to redefine tragedy are responses primarily to the 'death of tragedy' debate which, concomitant with discussions of the demise of the individual tragic hero in drama, has flourished since the eighteenth century and has resurfaced periodically, for instance in the United States, among other countries, during the 1920s and more recently in the decades following the Second World War. It has often been plagued by ahistoricism as a result of what Raymond Williams, in his *Modern Tragedy,* has called an 'extraordinarily powerful attachment to an absolute meaning of tragedy' (5). In works such as Joseph Wood Krutch's *The Modern Temper* (1929) and Francis Fergusson's *The Idea of a Theater* (1949), to name two which are relevant to this study, one can see evidence not only of a commitment to a prescriptive view of tragedy but also of a refusal to allow for variations in and transmutations of the genre. Indeed, among critics of modern tragedy, Aristotelians and neo-Aristotelians abound, and it is not unusual to find a discussion praising Miller's conformism to Aristotelian tenets or damning his lack of adherence to these strictures.

The 'death of tragedy', of course, is a phenomenon of a different order than the diminishing popularity of a form such as the sonnet; tragedy in its original form was and is still seen by both practitioners and critics as not only an aesthetic mode but also an expression of a particular philosophy of life. Even criticism that seemingly concentrates on formal aspects reaches beyond formalism. In the writings about tragedy one finds evidence of a concern with the nature of society and with the contemporary vision of humanity; behind disillusioned cries about the disappearance of a particular genre often lies a critique of modern civilization.

There are those traditionalist critics who believe that a world was lost, and a valuable view of life with it, when dramatic tragedy, as it was known to previous ages, ceased to exist. In the writings of Krutch and Fergusson, for instance, the critique of modern drama is tantamount to a disparaging view of a pluralistic, mass-oriented and mass-producing society which is seen as glorifying mediocrity, idealizing scientific progress and occupying itself with drawing grey pictures of the commonplace. With characteristic anachronism, both Krutch and Fergusson measure modern drama against classical and Shakespearean tragedy – Krutch fails to differentiate between the two modes – and against Aristotelian tenets.

The critics of modern tragedy who participated in the 'death of tragedy' debate during the thirties, forties, fifties and early sixties can be loosely classified in several basic categories representing the main approaches. The first one includes those who, taking classical tragedy as the ideal and often not discriminating between form and content, discuss tragedy's disappearance from a world in which values have disintegrated; Krutch in *The Modern Temper* and *'Modernism' in Modern Drama* (1953) and Fergusson in *The Idea of a Theater* are in this category. Although George Steiner's *The Death of*

Tragedy (1961), with its estimation of liberal/rationalist optimism as the main factor in the death of tragedy, does not share Krutch's and Fergusson's rigid conservatism, it is best categorized in this group. The second category is represented by those who believe that the 'classical' concept of tragedy need not be at odds with the modern outlook. For instance Mark Harris, in *The Case for Tragedy* (1932), responds directly to Krutch's challenge; John Gassner argues for a modified but nonetheless classically-based conception of tragedy in numerous articles during the fifties and the sixties, as does Elder Olson in his *Tragedy and the Theory of Modern Drama* (1961). Those who speak for a generic metamorphosis of classical tragedy, specifically the modern prevalence of the hybrid genre of tragicomedy, comprise the third category. A most notable example of this approach is Lionel Abel in *Metatheatre* (1963), exploring the effect on the theatre of post-Renaissance dramatic self-consciousness, and J. L. Styan in *The Dark Comedy* (1962). And finally, the fourth category includes those who see the historical necessity of a distinctly modern tragedy and offer a radical redefinition of the genre. For instance, Raymond Williams, in *Modern Tragedy* (1966, 1979), insists on viewing ordinary suffering in terms of tragedy and champions a socialistic reading of tragedy. The writers in the first four categories range from those whom John Gassner, in 'The Possibilities and Perils of Modern Tragedy', calls 'traditionalists' to those he calls 'liberals' (Corrigan, 1965, 405–17). The latter, including Gassner, are those who believe that tragedy may be redefined in consonance with contemporary ideas and still retain the essential features of the classical genre; the former are those who proclaim the death of tragedy as a result of unfavorable conditions, such as a lack of unified vision, faith and humanism. Gassner's classification excludes the radical solutions to the problem of modern tragedy, the beliefs that tragedy is an outmoded form of dramatic expression bearing relevance to neither modern life nor art and that tragedy must be completely redefined to suit contemporary ideas, if it is to have any meaning for today's stage.

The discussion about genre has been further complicated by the fact that the word 'tragedy' has acquired the sanctity of an honorific title, so that critics are often hesitant to bestow the hallowed term on plays dealing with ordinary life, with the 'common man' or even on those resorting to prose rather than poetry. Consequently, playwrights who have wished to be part of the tragic tradition but who have focused on the ordinary and the commonplace, and especially those who have opposed the necessary fatalism and mysticism of classical tragedy, have been faced with the problem of trying to reconcile contemporary ideas with traditional tragedy.

II

The careers of Maxwell Anderson (1888–1959), Eugene O'Neill (1888–1953), Tennessee Williams (1911–83) and Arthur Miller (b. 1915) collectively span the greater part of the twentieth century, and their plays represent a wide range of dramatic forms; irrespective of the diversity, they share an interest in modern redefinitions of tragedy. The attempts of these playwrights to re-examine dramatic tragedy and the meaning of heroism deserve some critical attention because they reflect a prevalent disillusionment with modern life as well as with commercial theatre and propose to offer new dramatic approaches to heroism.

O'Neill's dedication to recreating tragic drama of earlier ages needs no introduction. Maxwell Anderson, a now nearly forgotten figure, was important on the New York stage of the thirties when O'Neill's career was in eclipse. Anderson is one of the few American playwrights to write on the subject in *The Essence of Tragedy*. However, more than in these two figures who attempted to bring into an American milieu classical and Elizabethan tragedy, at least in its modified form, in such plays as *Mourning Becomes Electra*, *Desire under the Elms* and *Winterset*, I became interested in two representatives of the second generation – Tennessee Williams and Arthur Miller – and in their involvement with dramatic tragedy and heroism. Miller's *Death of a Salesman* has become for many critics the quintessential modern tragedy and by implication, one would assume, Willy Loman the representative modern tragic hero. Miller's many articles on tragedy and dramatic heroism of course make him the obvious choice for a study of modern tragedy. Tennessee Williams has had less to say in the few articles he has written on the theatre and art in general, but his theatrical practice also points to an interest in tragedy and certainly in the nature of heroism in the modern world. I focus primarily on the period between the forties and early sixties with some reference to the thirties. The ideas and dramatic practice of O'Neill, a figure of singular importance in terms of technical experimentation and theatrical iconoclasm in the modern American theatre, are understood as an important precedent for an essentially anti-modernist strain. The two late O'Neill plays explored here – *A Long Day's Journey into Night* and *The Iceman Cometh* – suggest a relationship between O'Neill and the following generation of playwrights in light of their approaches to redefinitions of traditional forms. Thus, despite fundamental ideological differences between such playwrights as O'Neill and Miller, the two share more in terms of their perceptions of the modern world and their ideas about dramatic heroism than could be presumed on the basis of a casual acquaintance with their plays and articles.[1]

I examine selected plays by Miller, Williams, Anderson and O'Neill, primarily from the forties to the early sixties – decades marked by a renewed critical interest in tragedy – in terms of four versions of heroism. Careful consideration of plays and essays of the period led me to devise four general categories within which I could examine versions of heroism. The categories – idealism, martyrdom, self-reflection and survival – describe the focus of the plays and point to a specific redefinition of heroism. In terms of dramatic action, they reflect an increasing order of subjectivism and a decreasing order of external action, related tendencies symptomatic of the contemporary spirit.

Prominent plays of the period by playwrights propounding an interest in the revival of tragedy emphasize individual action and view it in heroic terms. Similarly, a large section of American drama criticism dealing with tragedy places almost exclusive emphasis on character and on a psychological reading of action; it often evaluates the structural aspects of tragedy and the underlying ideology in terms of individual action. In accordance with this particular focus of modern American drama and dramatic criticism, I make the assumption that specific forms of heroism constitute the tragic experience in these plays and that tragedy is most often interpreted as a dramatization of heroism; specifically, it is reduced to personal heroism, interpreted in a liberal humanist manner.

III

Chapter 1, 'Heroism Reconsidered', is a discussion of the ideas of critics who have questioned the possibility of modern tragedy and even the viability of modern theatre, specifically Joseph Wood Krutch's and Francis Fergusson's ideas on the decline of the theatre.

Among the critics, it is the 'traditionalists' who are representative of the intellectual climate that provoked a renewed interest in tragic drama; however, it is the liberal spirit – often misguided in its optimistic insistence on the reconciliation between tragedy and the modern world view – that playwrights who write contemporary tragedies share. The chapter attempts, through an examination of various essays, to situate the playwrights in these discussions and define their ideas of tragedy and of heroism in the face of the 'death of tragedy' debate. In Chapter 2, 'Idealism as Heroism', the characters' idealism is seen as a basis and prerequisite for the subsequent concepts of heroism discussed here. In the plays examined, the playwrights dramatize the unresolved tension between the rationalistic/materialist vision and the tragic/idealistic vision, a conflict which has been at the center of many discussions on modern tragedy. Protagonists in these plays partake of heroism by virtue of their total dedication to an ideal.

Chapter 3, 'Martyrdom as Heroism', further explores the preceding version of heroism and examines the concept of martyrdom which has concerned such scholars of tragedy as Butcher and Martz and which, it seems, finds expression in the selected plays. In this approach, the protagonists are martyr figures either persecuted by the social group or, as is more often the case, haunted by their own sense of sin or transgression and seeking self-sacrifice. Here action takes the form of suffering and fortitude, rather than of active struggle.

Chapter 4, 'Self-reflection as Heroism', discusses the phenomena of inwardness and subjectivism in terms of heroic intensity. The heroic struggle is completely internalized as the self-conscious and self-dramatizing protagonists attempt to deal with their past and to give meaning to their present. It is often through the self-conscious artistic recreation of past events and through the reconstruction of a life that the protagonist is able to arrive at a self-definition. Since the action is internalized, suffering has to do with agonizing self-trial, confession and forgiveness. Chapter 5, 'Survival as Heroism', examines the idea of heroism in terms of simple endurance. The plays deal with a group of protagonists and with the heroism inherent in sustaining hope in the face of a hopeless situation; the spiritual malaise is overwhelming and the struggle to continue living constitutes the action.

I view the plays in light of the playwrights' writings on the theatre, on tragedy and heroism in particular. My method relies on an examination of reciprocal 'influence' of plays and conceptual writing. While I do not treat various essays as prescriptive documents, I consider the ideas in them serving as a framework for a discussion of the plays; conversely, I use the plays to illuminate the documents. Or in other words, the plays illustrate the general intellectual, artistic and moral climate, while the essays often describe it and respond to it directly. The dialogue that exists, at least in the academic world, between the play as text and the critical essay illuminates approaches to heroism.

The four versions of heroism provide four different but related ways of looking at the plays and at the playwrights' shared concerns. They are indicative not only of a perceived crisis, but also of an attempted solution. The protagonists in the plays may not be heroic in the conventional sense – they wield no power, have limited influence and often command little respect – but they share an intensity and a dedication which, for the playwrights, serve as evidence against the loss of value and as proof of human dignity and integrity. The catastrophes that befall many of these protagonists engage them in such intense suffering that their experiences rival those of traditional tragic heroes and confirm the dramatists' belief in the possibility of tragic expression.

The playwrights' efforts to revive tragic vision and redefine heroism in consonance with the contemporary spirit constitute a response to both the state of the theatre and the nature of the modern world. Specifically, the renewed emphasis on heroism and, more importantly, the insistence on heroism as a prerequisite of vital drama, seem to be part of a response to an all-encompassing crisis – spiritual, intellectual and aesthetic. Tragic drama is considered by critics and playwrights to be a potentially affirmative statement meant to counteract modern spiritual degeneration. It is precisely the perception of humanity's insignificance that compels the playwrights to offer dramatized instances of humanity's dignity, and it is the presumed faithlessness of modern life that invites reaffirmations of faith.

In his 'Introduction to the Collected Plays' Miller writes that:

> For a society of faith, the nature of death can prove the existence of the spirit, and posits its immortality. For a secular society it is perhaps more difficult for such a victory to document itself and to make itself felt, but conversely, the need to offer greater proof of the humanity of man can make that victory more real. (33)

Although their approaches may vary, Miller, Williams, Anderson and O'Neill share a desire to document in their dramas what they perceive to be indications of human potential for greatness in a world which they see as denying a fundamental human dignity. And it is these versions of dignity and greatness as well as redefinitions of the tragic experience that this book examines.

1
Heroism Reconsidered

Ever since Nietzsche declared that the advent of the analytical Socratic temper was responsible for the death of tragedy by suppressing the Dionysian spirit, analyses of the ideal tragic form have been accompanied by lamentations over its passing. There is a general consensus among those who claim that tragedies, as we have known them, can no longer be written that the rational temper is inimical to the creation of tragedy, that the scientific view of life is incompatible with the tragic view of life. For instance, in *Tragic Sense of Life* (1913), Unamuno argues that once the scientific spirit enters a people's life, some of the discrepancies between the actual material order of the world and the preferred ideal order are explained, others accepted as truths. Thus a people loses its sense of mystery and so, too, its 'tragic sense of life'. The writing of tragedy, Unamuno maintains, is the unintellectual manifestation of humanity's frustrations and also a remedy for them. The intellectualization of life engenders an unfavorable climate because it is, at one and the same time, too skeptical and overly confident; that is, it dares to question and probe.

For some critics skepticism is a sign of confidence, for others one of despair. The latter is the view of Joseph Wood Krutch in *The Modern Temper* (1929), an influential study of the contemporary American *Zeitgeist*, a chapter of which is devoted to tragedy. Krutch is relevant to the discussion because his anti-rationalist approach to the problem of modern dramatic tragedy, and to literature in general, is shared by many of his contemporaries, critics and playwrights alike. Krutch moralizes Nietzsche's amoral, aesthetic argument: in *The Birth of Tragedy* Nietzsche argued that the rationalist, analytical and scientific approach, with its resulting cheerful spirit, was 'the baneful virus of our society'(109); like a number of contemporary critics and playwrights, Krutch believes that relativism, skepticism and ultimately amorality are the components of rationalism. His ideas represent one important current of criticism which, in a revised form, is still with us. The anti-rationalism and even anti-intellectualism of this belief system, its overriding nostalgia, both aesthetic and moral, are to be found in many of the American attempts of the period, as well as the following decades, to revive the tragic genre. For this reason, Krutch's argument in *The Modern Temper* is worthy of scrutiny. Although the four playwrights under discussion – with the possible exception of Anderson – do not necessarily share Krutch's at times aggressive skepticism regarding science, and indeed all facets of intellectual life, some elements of his brand of anti-rationalism are to be found in their writings.[1]

Krutch maintains that modern science has shown that human beings are insignificant and that their morality is obsolete; science has been responsible for the great demystification that has occurred in all fields of human endeavour. From this unfortunate intrusion of 'truth' into the world of the imagination springs what Krutch calls 'the modern temper'. According to him, the modern rational temper has made it impossible for humanity to believe in God or in itself. Under the cold gaze of science, previously absolute morality has become an arbitrary human invention, he argues. Thus deprived of the guiding power of absolute ethics, we must

> rest content with the admission that though the universe which science deals with is the real universe, yet we do not and cannot have any but fleeting and imperfect contact with it; that the most important part of our lives – our sensations, emotions, desires and aspirations – take place in a universe of illusions which science can attenuate or destroy, but which it is powerless to enrich. (72)

He concludes that, as a result of this modern predicament and of the overwhelming crisis of faith, 'tragedies, in that only sense of the word which has any distinctive meaning, are no longer written' (118). Perhaps the single most important idea around which his discussion revolves is the concept of tragedy as the optimistic expression of a confident age revelling in the celebration of its own greatness. The unhappy ending in tragedy is a means to an end, the end being the restoration of order and the satisfaction that comes from seeing the heroic exercise of the will. He asserts that 'for the great ages tragedy is not an expression of despair but the means by which they saved themselves from it' (126). If, for instance, Hamlet's life is sacrificed, it is for a noble cause, he believes. The destruction of the individual hero does not of course preclude the continuation of the order. Indeed, he goes on to say, in tragedy 'we accept gladly the outward defeats which it describes for the sake of the inward victories which it reveals' (125). In other words, outward defeats are to be seen as indeces of inward victories.

In a remarkably confident sweeping generalization Krutch maintains that in the twentieth century there are no noble causes worthy of dramatic treatment; the modern age is inferior because we are incapable of the optimistic vision tragedy presupposes. Modern drama offers us a view only of remediable (always a term of derision for a critic like Krutch) temporary outward defeats but no inward victory. In other words, modern drama – starting with Ibsen – deals with correctable social problems, rather than with heroic actions, and it has an amelioristic attitude. Its tone is uninspiring because its focus is the commonplace and the petty, not the exceptional and the grand. Clearly, recognition and acceptance of remediability and of social ameliorism can lead one to the denial of the relevance of a tragic view or of the need for tragic expression; in Krutch's case, however, awareness of this aspect of modern society and modern drama leads to disparagement of all things rational, intellectual and scientific and, by implication, all things modern.

Those who share Krutch's ideas also tend to believe that contemporary pluralism – and democracy, one cannot help but suspect – has undermined the unified moral vision that is a prerequisite for the creation of successful tragedies. In *The Idea of a Theater* (1949) Francis Fergusson contends that:

> The analysis of the art of drama leads to the idea of a theater which gives it its sanction, and its actual life in its time and place. And when the idea of a theater is inadequate or lacking, we are reduced to speculating about the plight of the whole culture. (226)

Fergusson views the modern situation from the vantage point of a Sophoclean or a Shakespearean 'idea of a theater', which he, among others, maintains mirrored a widely shared set of beliefs and values upon which the dramatist could build an artistic vision. He believes that

> . . . we cannot understand the arts and the visions of particular playwrights, nor the limited perfection of minor dramatic genres,

> without some more catholic conception of the art in general. Thus the pious effort to appreciate contemporary playwrights leads behind and beyond them. It leads, I think, to the dramatic art of Shakespeare and the dramatic art of Sophocles, both of which were developed in theaters which focused at the center of the life of the community, the complementary insights of the whole culture. (1)

The Sophoclean and Shakespearean theatres provide models of the ideal theatre; Dante's *Divine Comedy,* for Fergusson the perfect exemplum of the Aristotelian idea of a 'complete imitation of action', towers above the entire discussion. According to Fergusson, Dante's great work displays 'the most developed idea of the theater of human life' (2), because it explores every imaginable aspect of both private and public life. Its epic totality of experience is something that is lacking in contemporary theatre.

Fergusson believes that although the 'centerless diversity of our theater may be interpreted as wealth' (2), the unfocused arbitrariness of much of modern drama is lamentable and results in the loss of a unified artistic perception of reality. The modern playwright's vision, finding expression in the narrow dramatic convention of social realism, is alienated even from the nature of contemporary reality. Fergusson maintains that in his own age it is impossible to conceive of a theatrical convention, of an idea of a theatre, that could speak to a specific, identifiable cultural community, that could progress beyond the dramatizing of a fragmented, relativistic vision of the world. He sees theatre as a mirror of society and referring to Hamlet's direction to the players 'to hold as 'twere the mirror up to nature', contends that if

> . . . [Hamlet] could ask the players to hold the mirror up to nature, it was because the Elizabethan theater was itself a mirror which had been formed at the center of the culture of its time, and at the center of the life and awareness of the community. (1–2)

In our protean age, on the other hand, 'such a mirror is rarely formed', he argues, because our age seems to lack definition: 'We are more apt to think of it as a wilderness which is without form' (1–2). Moreover, our understanding of human nature precludes the formation of a coherent and unified cultural vision, because:

> Human nature seems to us a hopelessly elusive and uncandid entity, and our playwrights . . . are lucky if they can fix it, at rare intervals, in one of its momentary postures, and in a single bright, exclusive angle of vision. Thus the *very* idea of a theater, as Hamlet assumed it, gets lost . . . . (2)

Like Krutch, always measuring the modern against the ancient, he despairs about the condition of contemporary society and understands the state of the theatre to be just one symptom in its general decline. The arguments put forth by Krutch and Fergusson are propelled by a perception – shared by Maxwell Anderson and Eugene O'Neill, and to some extent by Tennessee Williams, and even, at times, by Arthur Miller – of the loss of spiritual, and especially moral, dimension. When Krutch speaks of faithlessness, he is in fact speaking of what he understands to be a lack of moral conviction and an overwhelming loss of hope. Krutch states that the demise of the mythic and tragic vision is 'the result of one of those enfeeblements of the human spirit' and is another indication of the 'gradual weakening of man's confidence in his ability to impose upon the phenomenon of life an interpretation acceptable to his desires' (119).

Krutch begins his critique of the modern era by comparing the fate of humanity in the twentieth century to the fate of the child who grows up and leaves innocence behind forever. Modern man, he says, 'has exchanged the universe which his desires created, the universe made for man, for the universe of nature of which he is only a part' (8). As a consequence, humanity gradually developed from an anthropocentric sense of security and an unquestioning faith in the meaning of life to skepticism and insecurity. Rationalism has not only rendered traditional absolute morality untenable, it has failed to bring meaning and confidence into life.[2]

Krutch contends that the creation of tragedy presupposes a faith in humanity and a belief in mystery, which are no longer available to the modern world, and diagnoses the situation in the following manner:

> The structures which are variously known as mythology, religion, and philosophy, and which are alike in that each has its function the interpretation of experience in terms which have values, have collapsed under the force of successive attacks and shown themselves utterly incapable of assimilating the new stores of

> experience which have been dumped upon the world. With increasing completeness science maps out the pattern of nature, but the latter has no relation to the pattern of human needs and feelings. (12)

In other words, it does not seem possible to translate the vast scientific knowledge into a viable value system that would render the contemporary experience intelligible, and thus make modern life tolerable and modern drama interesting and relevant. Needless to say, the paucity of historical, political and social analysis in Krutch's critique renders his observations too vague to be useful and reduces them to the complaints of a man chronicling not so much the spirit of the age as his, and his colleagues', disenchantment. A sense of unidentified, general disillusionment of this kind with both intellectual and moral life underlies some of the attempts to revive tragedy, to engage in 'experiments' in old forms. In much the same vein as Krutch, Fergusson insists that a unifying cultural idea is indispensable for the maintenance of a theatrical tradition:

> Unless the cultural components of our melting-pot are recognized, evaluated, and understood in some sort of relationship – our religious, racial, and regional traditions, and our actual habits of mind derived from applied science and practical politics, seen as mutually relevant – how can we get a perspective on anything? And how can we hope for a public medium of communication more significant than that of our movie palaces, induction centers, and camps for displaced persons? (226–7)

It would seem from Fergusson's analysis that he considers the failure to superimpose an intelligible organizing principle on disparate cultural phenomena – as much as the fact of pluralism and fragmentation – to be responsible for the absence of a relevant theatre.

Maxwell Anderson shares Krutch's and Fergusson's belief that a ubiquitous collapse of values and a crisis of faith characterize modern life and that this must necessarily be reflected in the state of the theatre. In 1945 he writes in a letter that 'a good play cannot be written except out of conviction – for or against – and when convictions wobble the theatre wobbles' (*Dramatist in America*, 203–4). And yet, he is aware that optimism is difficult to maintain in the post-war world, because

> it's likely that there has never been such a general disintegration of beliefs and morals as now. Men and women, one and all, are in the unfortunate position of having to live by unproveable, improbable and generally nonsensical propositions which their busy, logical brains are constantly attacking and bringing to the ground. And when logic has won, and the man – or the civilization – is entirely cynical – then the man or civilization is ready for the eternal junk-pile. Novels and poems don't necessarily die at such a time. Novels can be made out of pure gossip; poems can be made out of pure despair. But a play cannot exist without some kind of affirmation. (203)

In an at best misguided and at worst dangerous rhetorical strategy, Anderson places 'logic' and rationalism – which in turn can breed cynicism, he believes – in direct opposition to 'hope', faith and optimism, and links the victory of rationalism and the modern reliance on science to a general disintegration of values and hence to pessimism. In the essay 'Whatever Hope We Have', he indicates that the culprit is 'mere scientific advance without purpose' (23). However, behind a warning against progress without purpose or a call for ethical responsibility in science lies Anderson's main concern with a loss of faith based on mystery and with an overwhelming reliance on science. Like Krutch, Anderson is essentially anti-scientific, not just critical of scientific ethics. He also records the overwhelming skepticism regarding faith, whether public or private, political or religious. It is interesting to note that, like others who use the state of the theatre as a gauge for the state of society, Anderson places drama in a special class of morally affirmative literature and theatre in the privileged category of a mirror of society. For his part, Anderson believes – and he has this in common with Eugene O'Neill and with Krutch – that any hope of renewed faith must be linked to a revival of tragedy, which he views as a viable organizing principle.

Twenty-four years after writing *The Modern Temper*, Krutch restates in *'Modernism' in Modern Drama* (1953) his contention that the creation of tragedy is dependent upon certain assumptions concerning the reality of the ego, the responsibility of the individual for his or her conduct, the dignity of the human being and his or her supreme importance in the universe (115–16). And it is a set of presumptions significantly different from these that underlies the 'modernist' spirit, namely: a radical break with the past, a sense of ethical relativity, an awareness of a delicate balance between sanity and insanity, and a sense of the mystery of human behaviour.

In the chapter 'How Modern is Modern American Drama?' Krutch points out the essentially 'classical' – as opposed to 'revolutionary' – nature of modernism in its late stages when it reaches the United States in the 1920s. That is, by this time, the formerly revolutionary tenets and practices have appropriated the solidity of tradition, and the movement has all but lost its provocative tone. It is this modified version of 'modernism' that, according to him, is prevalent in American literature. And, one may add, such diverse factors as commercial pressures, the very nature of the Broadway audience, the American penchant for optimism and moralizing have watered down this already thin version of the movement. If indeed it is a modernism, it is necessarily a consumers' modernism. Again, Krutch voices his anti-rationalist beliefs when he asserts that it is 'the quality of human experience', rather than a rational analysis of it, that theatre must explore if life is 'to seem worthy of respect and of admiration' (112). He goes on to describe the dramas of O'Neill and Anderson, both writers of tragedies and therefore, he says, anti-modernists. It is his belief

> that both represent a reaction against what I have described as 'modernism in drama' by virtue of the assumption, instinctive in O'Neill's case, more self-conscious in that of Anderson, that their response to the spectacle of human life is one which can best be expressed and communicated in the form most obviously implying faith in, as well as respect for, the human spirit. (117)

He views O'Neill's preoccupation with 'the relation of man to God' (118) and his dramatization of the search for something greater to which one can belong as evidence of the playwright's interest in the exploration of traditional tragic themes. Whether stressing the necessity for a religion or concentrating on the need for ethical standards, O'Neill and Anderson are 'anti-modernists', according to Krutch,

> not only upon the fact that both see the traditional form of tragedy as in itself a significant comment on a world which has lost its sense of human dignity but also upon the fact that both chose as the most important theme of their tragedies man's persistent desire to be noble in a sense which one

> dominant kind of rationalism insists does not really make sense. (123)

Krutch believes that these playwrights turn to tragedy because it seems to express most effectively their concerns for loss of value and for disintegration, and also to embody alternative visions. One should not forget, furthermore, that tragedy promises to bring not only grandeur but dramatic excellence to a moribund stage and while in an age of uninspired realism tragedy may appear to be a bold experiment, its traditional identity assures instant respect and safe fame for the playwright.

Using the criteria he applied to Anderson and O'Neill, Krutch also considers two of the later generation of playwrights – Miller and Williams – to be traditionalists. It is of course possible, he believes, to see *Death of a Salesman* or *A Streetcar Named Desire* in terms of modernist theatre; however, it is equally possible to see them in a totally different light: 'the brutal naturalism' of *Salesman* may give way to 'a study of the effects of moral weakness and irresponsibility'. According to this view, 'the moral of the play becomes a classical moral and must necessarily presume both the existence of the classical ego and the power to make a choice' (125). Similarly, he maintains that

> Williams, despite all the violence of his plays, despite what sometimes looks very much like nihilism, is really on the side of what modernists would call the Past rather than the Future – which means, of course on the side of those who believe that the future, if there is to be any civilized future, will be less new than most modern dramatists from Ibsen on have professed to believe. (129)

The problem with this analysis is that it seems to identify modernism with a type of futurism and anti-modernism with traditionalism. Furthermore, Krutch does not distinguish between form and content, and thus does not account for the possibility of using modernist techniques to attack modern ideas (in the manner of Eliot, for instance) or disguising modernist ideas in conventional form in order to make them palatable for the commercial market. In other words, it is possible to be a formal modernist and an ideological traditionalist and thus be on the side of the Past, a stance Krutch considers anti-modernist. Krutch of course claims that O'Neill and Anderson – and even Miller and Williams – turn to traditional forms, away from modernist forms of expression, and that they also look to the past for guidance and solace. To consider these American playwrights anti-modernist, solely by virtue of their frequently vague and undefined conservatism, is to simplify matters greatly.

In *A Streetcar Named Desire* Williams evokes a vision of a supposedly cultured, civilized past which clashes violently with a brutal, philistine present. However, his perspective on the past is much more complicated, his emotional relationship with it and his intellectual attitude to it more complex than Krutch implies. In fact, it is the ambiguity of that rapport and Williams' divided sympathies, as conveyed to the audience, that are responsible for the complexity of the figure of Blanche and for the audience's subtly shifting sympathies throughout the play. Although it is evident that Blanche is the victim, the playwright, as he admitted in a 1978 interview with Cecil Brown, can occasionally sympathize with Stanley's plight as well (*Conversations with Tennessee Williams*).[3] And of course if we approach the play sensitively and critically, what emerges is not a simple struggle between two opposing elements and a destruction of the weaker by the stronger, but a much more complex, carefully choreographed dance of two entities, at least one of which – that represented by Blanche – does not have a sharply defined outline and whose identity is formed and finally deformed by the other. Similarly, the relationship between past and present in the play has none of the clear-cut simplicity many commentators, especially early ones, assigned to it. After all, Blanche not only descends into the lower depths of the Kowalski household but simultaneously journeys into her past, her private hell of guilty conscience. The two journeys are one.

The violence in the play may be a function of the severing of an inhumane future from a meaningless past, but it is also a manifestation of a conflict between a past which still weighs heavily on the present and a future which is already taking shape. This violent drama is enacted both between the characters (in the form of the conflict between Blanche and Stanley) and within the main character (in Blanche's internal struggle with her own past). Rather than an unequivocal faith in and dependence on the past, what emerges from this play – and from others of the period – is the troubled relationship of the central character, and often by implication of America, to the past. In *A Streetcar Named Desire*, in

Death of a Salesman and in *The Glass Menagerie* the loss of the past is mourned, but those who desire the past (Willy, Blanche, Amanda) do not seem to be in control of their own present and are out of touch with reality. Although that reality is seldom desirable, the past is always a remembered past, coloured by desire and pain; judging by the mental instability of the protagonists, memory is not to be trusted. Much of the criticism that claims the simple opposition between past and present fails to see the conflict in the context of the dramatic structure. The plays under dicussion emphasize not so much a rupture between past and present as a confusion, an overlap and even the simultaneity of past and present. Williams is neither on the side of the 'Past', as Krutch would have it, nor on the side of the 'Future'. If anything, he dramatizes the inseparability of these concepts as they have been appropriated and internalized by his characters; he is more interested in human perceptions of past, present and future than in the Past and Future Krutch has in mind.[4]

In the twentieth century an interest in tragedy in many instances denotes an anti-modernist attitude not so much because it shows a siding with the Past, but rather because it indicates at once a faith in traditional values – specifically in fixed ethical and moral standards – a belief in determinate human nature and a degree of fatalism. This latter aspect is seldom stressed by critics such as Krutch, Fergusson, Miller or Anderson, but it is as much a part of the tragedy 'package' as the unconditional faith in an unchanging human nature. And it is this deterministic and fatalistic outlook that has made tragedy untenable for many playwrights and critics. For instance, throughout his career, Miller has struggled with the problem of tragedy's fatalism. On one hand, his social focus, his early quasi-Marxist analysis and amelioristic impulse are of course at odds with any determinism that tragedy may require. And yet, the socio-economic structures as he presents them in his plays are often shown to constitute a fate as fixed and predetermined as any we might encounter in traditional tragedy.

By contrast, O'Neill is attracted to the fatalism of tragedy. His dedication to tragic drama grows out of a recognition – influenced greatly by Nietzsche's writings, particularly *Thus Spake Zarathustra*[5] – of a modern crisis, the awareness of which is sharpened by a personal crisis of faith. Perturbed not only by the general loss of spiritual dimension but specifically by the American emphasis on material values, he attacks rampant materialism throughout the

1920s, most notably in plays such as *Marco Millions, The Fountain* and *Lazarus Laughed,* to name only three. At the same time, he believes that America is 'in the throes of a spiritual awakening' (Gelb and Gelb, 486–7) because, he says,

> A soul is being born . . . and when a soul enters, tragedy enters with it. Suppose some day we should suddenly see with the clear eye of a soul the true valuation of all our triumphant brass band materialism; should see the cost – and the result in terms of eternal verities. What a colossal, ironic, 100 per cent American tragedy that would be – what? Tragedy not native to our soil? Why, we are tragedy – the most appalling yet written and unwritten.

Denying the possibility of tragic expression would be, O'Neill insists, 'the most damning commentary on our spiritual barrenness' (486). For O'Neill, the challenge is to fill the spiritual vacuum in which he sees individuals and society suspended. And it is in the theatre that he finds the most profound expression of a spirituality that is missing in the modern world.

He strives to emulate Strindberg's intensified theatrical presentation, what O'Neill calls 'super-naturalism'; as he writes in the 1924 Playbill for *The Spook Sonata,*[6] he considers Strindberg 'among the most modern of moderns, the greatest interpreter in the theatre of the characteristic spiritual conflicts which constitute the drama – the blood – of our lives today' (Cargill, 108). To go beyond 'the banality of surfaces' and explore 'behind-life' (109) drama, as Strindberg had done, becomes his goal. The non-realistic, imaginative theatre he envisions and experiments with is to recall the ritual quality of the Dionysian Greek theatre; in 'Memoranda on Masks' he writes that the new theatre must be

> a theatre returned to its highest and sole significant function as a Temple where the religion of a poetical interpretation and symbolical celebration of life is communicated to human beings, starved in spirit by their soul-stifling daily struggle to exist as masks among the masks of living! (Cargill, 121–2)

This visionary theatre is to become a substitute for the religious communion that is lacking in O'Neill's life and, by extension, in modern life in general.

Anderson also places his faith in the theatre. The poet in the theatre becomes for him the ultimate seer, the glorifier of humanity and the saviour of a morally disintegrating world; Anderson believes that it is the modern stage, more than any other public forum, that has the potential for lifting humanity out of despair. He writes in 'A Prelude to Poetry in the Theatre' that the theatre 'has the power to weld and determine what the race dreams into what the race will become' (36) because, he says in 'The Essence of Tragedy', 'at its best it is a religious affirmation, an age-old rite restating and reassuring man's belief in his own destiny and his ultimate hope' (14).[7]

An incorrigible optimist, Anderson writes in 'Yes, By the Eternal' that the playwright must go counter to all material evidence and must show humanity endowing its meaningless world with meaning and creating order out of disorder. Like Krutch, he sees tragedy as embodying mankind's youthful 'hope that man is greater than his clay, that the spirit of man may rise superior to physical defeat and death' (51), and in such plays as *Key Largo, Elizabeth the Queen* and *Journey to Jerusalem* attempts to create dramas that affirm individual greatness and dignity.

In 'The Essence of Tragedy', his 'modern version of Aristotle' (8), Anderson places foremost emphasis on his own reinterpretation of *anagnorisis*, the Aristotelian concept of recognition. He postulates that 'the essence of tragedy, or even of a serious play, is the spiritual awakening, or regeneration of . . . [the] hero' (10) consisting of 'a discovery . . . of some element in his environment or in his soul of which he has not been aware – or which he has not taken sufficiently into account' (6). This central crisis must result in a complete altering of the course of the action and propel the hero toward the spiritual awakening that is the proper end of tragedy. In Aristotle's *Poetics, anagnorisis* refers to 'a change from ignorance to knowledge' (Butcher, 41). The ideal form of recognition, Aristotle contends, 'is coincident with a Reversal of the Situation, as in the Oedipus' (41). He defines *peripeteia*, reversal of situation, as

> a change by which the action veers around to its opposite, subject always to our rule of probability or necessity. Thus in the Oedipus, the messenger comes to cheer Oedipus and free him from his alarms about his mother, but by revealing who he is, he produces the opposite effect. (41)

There are various kinds of recognition, involving persons, things or events; however, it is recognition of persons, Aristotle maintains, that 'is most intimately connected with the plot and action' and, as a result, 'combined with reversal, will produce either pity or fear' (41). Thus recognition of personal identity leads directly to the ironic reversal of fortune.

Anderson understands recognition to mean self-recognition, that is the self-knowledge that is the result of self-examination. In his moralized scheme, recognition is directly linked to spiritual enlightenment and the awakening of moral consciousness; appropriately, the development 'from ignorance to knowledge' usually has to do with a burgeoning of faith and with a growing awareness of moral responsibility. For instance, in *Key Largo*, King McCloud 'recognizes' that to preserve his humanity, he must create his own faith in the midst of faithlessness. This recognition or discovery leads to his spiritual awakening and to a course of action which will mean his moral triumph and his physical destruction.

It is evident that both Anderson and O'Neill see the theatre as embodying a quasi-religious function in a faithless age. Metaphysical concerns provide a transcendant interest to a drama hitherto dealing only with material realities. This larger focus is an attempt, at one and the same time, to surpass the limitations of realism and to overcome the emphasis on materialism. The playwrights who have sought to keep alive tragedy, or revive it, tend to believe that the persistence of the tragic vision is a testament to the indestructibility of the human spirit. Tragedy expresses the spiritual malaise, but by its very existence in fact denies it. Furthermore, they identify the genre with a psychological, moral and ethical intensity lacking in modern life. Williams, for instance, has said in 'The Timeless World of the Play' that tragedy has a heightening and a sharpening effect, for it presents 'a world of fiercely illuminated values in conflict' (54) or 'in violent juxtaposition' (53). Despite radical differences between him and Miller, Williams' statement bears some resemblance to Miller's assertion, in 'The Nature of Tragedy', that the tragic mode brings about an 'illumination of the ethical' (9) and 'a more exalted kind of consciousness' (10). Whereas Miller stresses tragedy's potential to lift drama into a consciously moral realm, Williams' emphasis is on metaphysical contemplation and aesthetic transcendance of temporarity that dramatic art affords. Time and change are the enemies of human dignity, Williams says in 'The Timeless World of the Play', for 'it is [the] continual rush of time, so violent that it appears to be screaming, that deprives our actual lives of so much dignity and meaning' (49). The act of aesthetic creation captures the eternal and safeguards the characters and the action against the ravages of time. Williams believes that it is 'the *arrest of time* which has taken place in a completed work of art that gives to certain plays their feeling of depth and significance' (49). The 'timeless' universe of drama 'is removed from that element which makes people *little* and their emotions fairly inconsequential' (51).

The problem with Williams' idea of the timeless nature of art is that he applies a romantic, lyrical concept to drama. Although all literary, visual and plastic art may be 'eternal' in the obvious sense that it outlives its creator, theatrical presentation is timebound and while it redefines time – or creates its own time which invades the time of the spectators – it is not a static artform of the kind to which the Keatsian sentiment could be applied. In a sense, a dramatic work is never 'completed' and time in it is not arrested. What we find in drama is not the moment frozen in an aesthetic eternity, but the constant enactment and re-enactment of an action, existing in time and space – fluid and continuous, and different with each re-enactment. Thus perhaps it is not 'timelessness' or the 'arrest of time' that is the source of significance but rather continuity through endless re-enactments.

For Williams' protagonists, the struggle against meaninglessness has to do not only with acts of faith, but also with a combat against time, or aging and death. Williams believes that humanity can endow its meager and fated existence with meaning through the aesthetic examination of existential truths. He writes in 'The Timeless World of the Play' that:

> The great and only possible dignity of man lies in his power to deliberately choose certain moral values by which to live as steadfastly as if he, too, like a character in a play, were immured against the corrupting rush of time. Snatching the eternal out of the desperately fleeting is the great magic trick of human existence. As far as we know, as far as there exists any kind of empiric evidence, there is no way to beat the game of *being* against *non-being,* in which non-being is the predestined victor on realistic levels. (52)

Translating this emphasis on the aesthetic transformation of reality into the fabric of drama, in plays such as *Orpheus Descending, Cat on a Hot Tin Roof* and *A Streetcar Named Desire*, among others, Williams focuses on a person of special sensibility who undertakes the tragic resistance against the corruption of time. Indeed, the act of resisting corruption and decay is inextricably tied to the attempt to remain oblivious to time; for instance, Brick Pollitt's refusal to participate in life (in *Cat on a Hot Tin Roof*) represents a rejection not only of moral degeneration and societal hypocrisy – what Brick calls 'mendacity' – but also of temporal change, through the rejection of procreation. (After all, as Temple reminds us in *A Portrait of the Artist as a Young Man*, reproduction is the beginning of death.) For Brick procreating is tantamount to giving in to Maggie's wish to be part of the life cycle, in the play presided over by Big Daddy, representative of growth, change, decay and death.

The attempt to recapture a time of innocence, a time before the decisive choice was made, is at the center of a number of protagonists' quests: it is this that drives Blanche DuBois, Willy Loman and Mary Tyrone (in *Long Day's Journey into Night*) to destruction; it is also the only thing that sustains them through an adherence to a life-giving illusion. In order to challenge the existing situation, to confront their fate, the heroic protagonists must cling to their illusions. In *A Streetcar Named Desire, Death of a Salesman, All My Sons, Long Day's Journey into Night* and *Cat on a Hot Tin Roof*, for instance, it is the shattering of illusions that signals the hero's or heroine's ruin.

Krutch, like many others, attributes the demise of tragedy to a loss of illusion, among other factors. According to him, human beings are no longer the mystery they had been; every aspect of their body, mind and soul has been explored by science. And since no illusions remain, belief in human nobility and moral fortitude are no longer conceivable. The plays we describe as tragic, he says, have nothing in common with earlier forms of tragedy. Indeed, he points out in *The Modern Temper*, that they

> produce in the reader a sense of depression which is the exact opposite of the elation generated when the spirit of a Shakespeare rises joyously superior to the outward calamities which he recounts and celebrates the greatness of the human spirit whose travail he describes. (118–19)

The elation Krutch attributes to Greek and Elizabethan tragedy, and which he finds lacking in modern tragedy, is not a Nietzschean metaphysical joy but rather an optimistic moral affirmation. According to Nietzsche, by asserting the unity of life, the destruction of the hero (who belongs to the phenomenal world) leads to an affirmation, to that 'metaphysical solace' which tells the spectator that 'despite every phenomenal change, life is at bottom indestructibly joyful and powerful' (50). Like some of his contemporaries, Krutch repeatedly speaks of the greatness of the human spirit, rather than of the nature of existence. In other words, he – like the American dramatists discussed here – focuses on what he believes to be tragedy's glorification of the individual and its celebration of human potential, rather than on its dramatization of existential issues and its fatalistic outlook.

For Krutch, and for these playwrights, emphasis on psychological aspects of characterization and moral focus on personal faith are central to an understanding of tragic affirmation and heroism. O'Neill, among others, is skeptical about de-individualizing stylization in the theatre. Although he admires the dynamism of expressionistic theatre, in a 1924 interview he equates expressionism with the dramatization of types, not individuals, and comments that it 'denies the value of characterization' (Cargill, 111). Because the audience cannot identify with abstractions, 'it loses the human contact by which it identifies itself with the protagonist of the play' (111), he argues. Nonetheless, he believes that he had succeeded in blending expressionist technique with psychological realism in *The Hairy Ape*: Yank 'remains a man and everyone recognizes him as such' (111), says O'Neill; Yank is both a man and a symbol of Man in his struggle with fate. O'Neill's ideas on the use of masks attest to his emphasis on subjectivism and on the exploration of psychological states. As he says in 'Memoranda on Masks', for him, 'the new psychological insight into human cause and effect [is] a study in masks, an exercise in unmasking' (116). The masks do not conceal the real face but rather reveal that reality which is usually obscured by the 'maskless' face; they are 'a symbol of inner reality' (117). It is evident that the purported function of the mask is to bring into sharper focus the subjective vision, rather than to stylize and objectify or to dramatize abstract forces. This concern with psychological realism and with audience empathy is shared by Anderson, Miller and Williams. Indeed, Anderson's insistence on moral illumination, O'Neill's dramatization of the individual's lost battle against Fate, Miller's focus in 'Tragedy and the Common

Man' on 'the indestructible will of man to achieve his humanity' (7), Williams' preoccupation with artistic temperaments and people of heightened moral sensibility in a decaying materialistic world, all indicate a continued emphasis on the exploration of character, on the search for a viable definition of heroism in the modern world and on defining tragedy solely in terms of individual struggle and suffering.

In spite of their frequently voiced intention to confront the metaphysical realm and deal with existential issues, these playwrights seldom create what Jean-Paul Sartre, in his 1946 essay 'Forgers of Myths', refers to as 'theatre of situation', a moral, ritualistic theatre derived from the Aristotelian idea of primacy of action and dramatizing 'the conflict of rights' (332). In 'Forgers of Myths', an article occasioned by the New York critics' uninformed reactions to a performance of Jean Anouilh's *Antigone,* Sartre offers American audiences an insight into the new post-war theatre of France, into its social and philosophical attitudes and dramatic practices. Although he announces a return to classical traditions, or rather a critical re-examination of them, he dismisses any interest in the much debated 'return to tragedy' because he considers tragedy 'an historic phenomenon which flourished between the sixteenth and eighteenth centuries' and which the playwrights have 'no desire to begin . . . over again' (324). Nor is the contemporary French dramatist interested in bringing back philosophic plays if by these is meant the methodical treatment of philosophical doctrines, Sartre explains.

A 'great collective, religious phenomenon' (330) is what Sartre believes the theatre should be; this is not to say, however, that his understanding of the communal nature of drama bears any resemblance to O'Neill's or to Anderson's concept of the theatre as a place where faith in humanity can be reaffirmed through explorations of individual psychology and personal ethical dilemmas. Rather, he states that the new playwrights have made a break with the pre-war tradition of theatre of characters, which still dominates Broadway; they dramatize the great myths, the archetypal situations. (And it is, of course, as a consequence of this preoccupation with character analysis that the New York critics failed to interpret correctly the figure of Antigone who is a force, pure will, rather than an individual with complex distinguishable psychological traits.)

Sartre explains in the 'Forgers of Myths' that the new generation – Anouilh, Camus, de Beauvoir and Sartre himself – see the individual as

> a free being, entirely indeterminate, who must choose his own being when confronted with certain necessities such as being already committed in a world full of both threatening and favorable factors among other men who have made their choices before him, who have decided in advance the meaning of those factors. . . . That is why we feel the urge to put on the stage certain situations which throw light on the main aspects of the condition of man and to have the spectator participate in the free choice which man makes in these situations. (325)

Therefore, taking as their starting point the indeterminacy of human nature and the existential freedom confronting each individual, the new playwrights dramatize existential affirmation through their *dramatis personae*'s self-definition.

This 'austere, moral, mythic, and ceremonial' (335) theatre, as Sartre calls it, is a response to a twentieth-century, and particularly post-war, malaise. It posits affirmation in the discovery of archetypal paradigms. The O'Neillian search for a new 'god' has its parallel in what Sartre describes as explorations of 'moral and metaphysical topics [which] reflect the preoccupation of a nation which must at one and the same time reconstruct and recreate and which is searching for new principles' (335). However, unlike O'Neill, Satre is referring to social, political and philosophical principles, not spiritual ones. Myth serves as an organizing principle, and it is the characters who play out the archetypal situations, rather than the situations which enhance the character portrayal.

By contrast, the playwrights discussed here usually emphasize the psychological delineation of character and individual heroism. Tragedy is often tantamount to a dramatization of heroism, albeit redefined in consonance with contemporary requirements and perceptions of individualism. As a result of this primary importance of character and psychological veracity, the question of the protagonist's social stature still has significance.

It is a critical commonplace that the democratizing process and the mechanical nature of the modern world have put an end to individual heroism on a grand scale, with the result that the protagonist has become an inarticulate and pathetic victim incapable of the moral enlightenment that tragedy requires. For instance, Krutch's concern with the modern loss of spiritual dimension is closely tied to his conviction that tragedy requires a noble hero, preferably of high social standing. He insists that the nobility of tragic heroes is symbolic; that is, it shows their inward majesty, not only their social and political status. Thus the gradual democratization in drama points to a diminishing belief in human greatness.

The discussion about the social stature of the tragic hero is central to an understanding of tragedy and heroism, even after two centuries of middle-class drama; consequently, Miller feels the need to defend his 'low' man's heroism and to argue for the validity of the common man as hero in his articles 'Tragedy and the Common Man' and 'Introduction to the Collected Plays'. In the latter, he recalls that he had always considered *Death of a Salesman* heroic and was perplexed by academic debates on the question of Willy's heroism, particularly by the decidedly anachronistic nature of the discussion which gauged heroism in terms of Greco-Elizabethan standards and ignored modern realities (31).

For Miller, stature still remains a necessary requisite of tragedy; however, he now defines it not in terms of social status, or even of mental or moral superiority, but rather in terms of the heroes' or heroines' intensities, their will to break out of the bounds imposed upon them, usually by society. He points out in the 'Introduction to the Collected Plays' that:

> There is a legitimate question of stature here, but none of rank, which is so often confused with it. So long as the hero may be said to have had alternatives of a magnitude to have materially changed the course of his life, it seems to me that in this respect at least, he cannot be debarred from the heroic role. (32)

In other words, the potential for heroism exists whenever the individual has sufficient control over his or her life to bring about significant change and also catastrophic consequences. Both the change and the catastrophe are of course delimited by the nature of modern life and by the circumscribed field of action in which the protagonists function.

Willy Loman's actions and their consequences will necessarily be of a different magnitude than those of King Lear; nonetheless, this does not mean that they will be less significant, since

> the less capable a man is of walking away from the central conflict of the play, the closer he approaches a tragic existence. In turn, this implies that the closer a man approaches tragedy the more intense is his concentration of emotion upon the fixed point of his

> commitment, which is to say the closer he approaches what in life we call fanaticism. ('Introduction to the Collected Plays', 7)

Thus tragic potential has to do with a total dedication which results in the hero's or heroine's destruction. Susanne Langer's description, in 'The Tragic Rhythm', of the tragic protagonist's intensified response and resulting self-destruction aptly characterizes this total dedication:

> . . . the protagonist grows mentally, emotionally, or morally, by the demand of the action, which he himself initiated, to the complete exhaustion of his powers, the limit of his possible development. He spends himself in the course of the one dramatic action . . . his entire being is concentrated in one aim, one passion, one conflict and ultimate defeat. (Corrigan, 90)

Miller champions ordinary humanity as legitimate subjects of tragedy and representatives of heroism, but implied in his discussion is a general skepticism, not unlike that of traditionalist critics such as Krutch or Fergusson, regarding the possible identity of the modern tragic hero. He, too, decries the dearth of moral affirmation – although he subscribes to a different morality than either Krutch or Fergusson – and the lack of a larger framework. Clearly, Miller's quarrel is not with pluralism or with the lack of a unified artistic vision, but rather with the dissociation of social and private identity in modern life and with the exclusive emphasis in the theatre on psychological causation. Although Miller stands in a different ideological camp than O'Neill or Williams, he is no less preoccupied than they are with dramatizing fragmentation and valuelessness.

However, unlike Krutch, he believes that the gradual diminution of the dramatic protagonist can be corrected not through a return to aristocratic tragedy, but through an introduction of historical and socio-political consciousness into the drama. In other words, the 'social play' must be reintroduced to a stage now dominated by an impoverished theatre of psychological explorations. Not only is social drama (so often erroneously equated with photographic realism) compatible with tragedy, he says, it is in fact the only kind of drama that can be truly tragic, for it broaches the potentially tragic issues of the modern era: the survival of the individual in a society which has appropriated the characteristics of Fate. He maintains that Greek tragedy was social drama *par excellence,* for it was a drama of the whole person. For a writer such as Miller, the social focus can only enlarge the frame of reference, rather than narrow it, as Krutch assumes, because it confronts the problem of social limitations and of individual attempts to transcend them. The social play, Miller believes, is a drama that encompasses a person's private life as well as his or her social identity and moves beyond individual psychological analysis to larger issues of social or existential significance.

Miller's identification of tragedy with social drama and definition of the social play in terms of tragedy bespeak his ties with the bourgeois tradition of the eighteenth century. His moralizing and social ameliorism in fact place him in the mainstream of the liberal tradition with its origin in sentimental social tragedy. His ideas of tragedy often resemble those of the eighteenth century, an era which saw the decline, or at least the considerable redefinition, of the genre and its deterioration into sentimental domestic drama. Interestingly enough, he resorts to some of the arguments used, among others, by George Lillo in *The London Merchant.* For both the eighteenth-century and the twentieth-century playwright, the wide audience appeal of the ordinary protagonist legitimizes the play's commonplace focus. It is an 'evident truth', says Lillo:

> . . . that tragedy is so far from losing its dignity, by being accommodated to the circumstances of the generality of mankind, that it is more truly august in proportion to the extent of its influence, and the numbers that are properly affected by it. As it is more truly great to be the instrument of good to many, who stand in need of our assistance, than to a very small part of that number. (3)

Linda Loman's famous 'Attention must be paid . . . ' speech, in *Death of a Salesman,* harks back as much to Lillo's plea (in his 1731 dedicatory essay to *The London Merchant*) as to Miller's socialist roots in the 1930s. Any partisan ideologizing on the part of Linda would of course be both unconvincing rhetoric and bad theatre; however, one gets the distinct feeling that in this speech Linda sums up Miller's ideas on the 'common man' in life and on stage. Willy seems to be a victim not so much of specific economic conditions at a particular historical time, but simply an ostensibly insignificant person whose real significance lies in the fact that he is a human being and therefore worthy of attention. In other words, Linda's speech says no less and no more than Lillo's similar plea for democratization. In *The Theater Essays* Miller relies on a comparable strategy in arguing for the appropriateness of the 'common man' as tragic subject.

Miller takes the separation of public and private realms in both life and drama as his starting point in his discussion about social plays and posits tragic suffering and heroism in the struggle to change the social environment. Tragedy, he maintains in 'Tragedy and the Common Man', is 'the consequence of a man's total compulsion to evaluate himself justly' (5). At the same time, he recognizes that continued emphasis on the antagonism between individual and society has resulted in the normalization of asocial attitudes and ultimately in an aesthetic dead-end. Consequently, he states in his essays on the theatre his dedication to balancing social and psychological causation in his plays.

The social play as Miller defines it rescues humanity from the solipsistic vision of a segment of modern drama. (Of course much of what Miller states in the essays is not necessarily reflected in his plays; in this Miller is no different from any artist who writes about art.) It also has the potential to remedy the phenomenon of the diminishing stature of modern protagonists by extending their sphere of action and influence into the public domain. Miller believes, as he states in 'Morality and Modern Drama', that

> the truly great work is the work which will show at one and the same time the power and force of the human will working with and against the force of society upon it. (203)

His emphasis in the early plays is social, earning him the reputation of social dramatist; specifically, it is an examination of late capitalist society and its objectification of people.

All My Sons and *Death of a Salesman* deal with various forms of alienation inherent in the economic system and with the deterministic nature of the social structure. Despite the mildly leftist overtones of *Death of a Salesman,* the play's relentless fatalism is an early indication of the direction Miller's later drama is to take. Similarly, while the play dramatizes the tragedy of a solipsistic existence, it resorts to and relies on solipsistic techniques (on a highly subjective theatrical presentation) to carry its ideas. In this play, the individuals are tragic playthings of a fate no less cruel and pitiless than that of the Greeks, for they are now no more than commodities, objects of commercial transaction of little intrinsic worth beyond their market value.

Throughout his early career, Miller remains torn between a firm commitment to social drama and an impulse to explore psychological states and to delve into ultimate meanings. Although he insists on the importance of social drama and of viewing the individual as a social product, Miller invariably depicts the tragedy of the loss of private integrity in the face of social pressure. His focus is social, but his perspective is always individualistic.

What is at stake in plays such as *All My Sons, Death of a Salesman* or *The Crucible* is not the survival of society or of a greater order but the integrity of the individual. *All My Sons* deals with the quest of a morally possessed son and the anguish of a guilty father who had betrayed him. As Eric Mottram, one of the few critics to comment on Miller's deterministic attitude to socio-political issues, points out in his essay on Miller's political ideology, the social conditions which had produced this situation remain unexamined, and any criticism levelled at social relationships is propelled by a concern for the individual not the group. According to Mottram, in Miller's plays the social structure remains

> uncondemned and unanalysed, taken as if it were an unchangeable artefact. The weight of action falls cruelly on the individual within the fixed, powerful society which fails to support him at his moment of need and remains, as he falls, monolithically immovable. (Corrigan, 1969, 23–4)

Similarly, the meaning of evil goes unexamined, Mottram maintains; it is simply presented in terms of 'those social pressures which conflict with an equally vaguely defined individual integrity in the hero or heroine'. In *All My Sons* and in *Death of a Salesman* the family melodrama, the revenge motive and the archetypal father/son conflict, culminating in the suicide-patricide, form the core of the play. Chris' and Linda's set speeches about social responsibility are invariably overshadowed by the issue of guilt.

Like O'Neill and Anderson, Miller in 'Tragedy and the Common Man' posits that the tragic feeling arises when protagonists struggle to define themselves and are ready to pay with their life for a sense of personal dignity:

> From Orestes to Hamlet, Medea to Macbeth, the underlying struggle is that of the individual attempting to gain his 'rightful' position in his society. (4)

Individuals are defined in terms of their society, but their tragic struggle has to do with their attempt to create their own identity, separate from the social mask. Underlying Miller's discussion about heroic stature is the assumption that ordinary persons – albeit their extraordinary representatives – have the ability, means and opportunity to shape and reshape their world. But even Miller concedes that the democratization of the tragic hero must necessarily lead to the relativization of heroism, or at least to a radical rethinking of its terms.

In much of modern drama, Miller agrees with Krutch, something is lacking. In his essay 'On Social Plays' the playwright states:

> In the heroic and tragic time the act of questioning the-way-things-are implied that a quest was being carried on to discover an ultimate law or way of life which would yield excellence; in the present time the quest is that of a man made unhappy by rootlessness and, in every important modern play, by a man who is essentially a victim. We have abstracted from the Greek drama its air of doom, its physical destruction of the hero, but its victory escapes us. (59)

In other words, contemporary tragedy has superficially adopted the form of Greek drama without its content and will be neither great theatre nor particularly representative of the era until it discovers a specifically modern significance.

In an attempt to reintroduce the grandeur of Greek tragedy to the American stage, O'Neill seeks to dramatize the eternal struggle of individuals against their Fate; to this end, he writes in a letter to Arthur Hobson Quinn, he is intent upon 'trying to interpret Life in terms of lives, never just lives in terms of character' (Quinn 2: 199). He considers himself 'a most confirmed mystic' and admits that he is

> always acutely conscious of the Force behind – (Fate, God, our biological past creating our present, whatever one calls it – Mystery, certainly) – and of the one eternal tragedy of Man in his glorious, self-destructive struggle to make the Force express

> him instead of being, as an animal is, an infinitesimal incident in its expression. (199)

His characters strive to understand their past in their struggle to belong to something outside themselves, something larger that would provide meaning. In this struggle against Fate the individual is always the loser, for 'the only success is in failure' (Gelb and Gelb, 337), but attains heroic stature in the hopeless battle.

O'Neill's understanding of spiritual victory and of optimism is central to his idea of tragic drama. In a 1921 article, 'Damn the Optimists!', he equates tragedy with a 'higher optimism':

> There is a skin deep optimism and another higher optimism, not skin deep, which is usually confounded with pessimism. To me, the tragic alone has that significant beauty which is truth. It is the meaning of life – and the hope. The noblest is eternally the most tragic. (Cargill, 104)

Nobility and tragic heroism have to do with a hopeless battle which ends in defeat but also in an ultimate moral victory. The human condition, O'Neill believes, is tragic, and tragedy perhaps its only significance (Gelb and Gelb, 336).

Miller had at one time been puzzled by O'Neill's much quoted statement about his interest in the relation of man to God (Krutch 'Introduction' *Nine Plays*, xvii). However, he later conceded that tragedy must transcend not only narrow psychological confines and limiting emphasis on the individual but even social analysis, and must broach questions of existential import. Like O'Neill, he believes that struggle makes the protagonist noble; unlike O'Neill, Miller still speaks of an ongoing, not necessarily failed, social struggle, rather than a spiritual one. Although he, too, believes in a force larger than humanity and often hostile to it, he places the sense of fate in social and economic determinism. And even this is not fixed; rather, it is, as he writes in the 'Introduction to the Collected Plays', an everchanging process affected by people:

> The history of man is a ceaseless process of overthrowing one determinism to make way for another more faithful to life's changing relationships . . . Any determinism, even the most scientific, is only that stasis, that seemingly endless pause, before the application of man's will administering a new insight into causation. (54)

Therefore, in the 'Introduction to the Collected Plays', he announces his intention of striking a balance between determinism and free will, of creating a drama which discovers and proves 'that we are made and yet are more than what made us' (55). This tension between a fixed order and freedom is echoed also in his desire to write tragedy and in the paradoxical need to ground his plays in historical and political specificity.

He writes in 'Tragedy and the Common Man' that the dominant force in the tragic situation is indignation which drives the protagonist to question the previously unquestioned, to attack the seemingly stable environment. It is the resulting disruption of order in a quest for meaning, often at the expense of the hero's life, that constitutes heroism:

> . . . in this stretching and tearing apart of the cosmos, in the very action of so doing, the character gains 'size', the tragic stature which is spuriously attached to the royal or the highborn in our minds. (6)

It is not the actual social status of the protagonist that matters, that ensures heroic grandeur, but rather, he says in the 'Introduction to the Collected Plays', 'the intensity, the human passion to surpass . . . given bounds' (33). However, the struggle of the protagonist must have more than individual significance. Miller argues that to have heroic stature, the ordinary person must act in a manner that implicates others; his or her actions must address

> the issues of, for instance, the survival of the race, the relationships of man to God – the questions, in short, whose answers define humanity and the right way to live so that the world is a home, instead of a battleground or a fog, in which disembodied spirits pass each other in an endless twilight. (32)

Although heroism is relative to the limited, but nonetheless ennobling, choices the protagonists make within their given possibilities, it has wider significance. Thus Willy Loman's or Blanche DuBois' choices and subsequent suffering place them in the heroic role despite their 'low' status in terms of the expectations of traditional tragedy. It is the playwrights who bestow 'greatness' upon their characters. Williams, for instance, admits in his *Memoirs* that he writes

> so often of people with no magnitude, at least on the surface. I write of 'little people'. But are there 'little people'? I sometimes think there are only little conceptions of people. (234)

Intensity, the capacity for suffering, is what gives characters 'size'. O'Neill's comment on his choice of protagonists is illustrative of a shared tendency. Apparently, he always tried 'to see the transfiguring nobility of tragedy, in as near the Greek sense as one can grasp it, in seemingly the most ignoble, debased lives' (Quinn 199). Underlying this statement is the understanding that characters need not be inherently noble but that suffering gives them dignity. According to her creator, Blanche DuBois 'was a demonic creature, the size of her feeling was too great for her to contain without the escape of madness' (*Memoirs*, 235). It is precisely this overabundance of feeling – together with a heightened sense of integrity and justice – that propels to a tragic end not only Blanche, but also Willy Loman, King McCloud (*Key Largo*) and Val Xavier (*Orpheus Descending*), to name only a few. And it is these characters' anguished surpassing of the common concerns and their reaching for the unattainable that elevates them above the rest; their doomed struggle against their own insignificance and against meaninglessness and their refusal to remain as ordinary as fate had decreed them to be endow them with dignity.

Those who perceive themselves as writers of tragedy attempt to establish new criteria for heroism in consonance with their own re-interpretations of contemporary reality. Miller, Williams, Anderson and O'Neill admit that contemporary heroism must necessarily be of a relative, diminished kind, the action often played out against a mundane background and the issues relatively banal. Nonetheless, these playwrights believe that a dramatic universe where conflicts between an inner world of conscience and an outer world of social reality are still conceivable, where sacrifices to ideals are still possible, in effect denies accusations of spiritual vacuity and affirms, if not greatness, then at least dignified ambiguity. Therefore they engage in the dramatic elevation of anguish and the romanticization of suffering in plays often only verging on tragedy or making only vague references to the genre, as they dramatize total personal dedication to an ideal.

Library of
Davidson College

2

Idealism as Heroism

Those who decry the lack of shared values in twentieth-century society and what they see as a resultant nihilism, are often perturbed by the loss of traditional values and of a particular view of life; specifically, they seem to disapprove of social, political, ethical and aesthetic pluralism. Furthermore, as in the case of Krutch and Anderson, they do not recognize that the advent of science may have brought about new forms of faith and confidence in humanity. Indeed, it is precisely these new forms of faith to which Nietzsche attributed the demise of tragedy, first in the Socratic era and then in his own time. In a comparable manner, the Marxists' optimism and social 'ameliorism', having as its ultimate vision the revolutionary restructuring of society, has made Marxists wary of literary tragedy. Similarly, the Christian world-view, with its promise of an after-life and divine compensation, is often seen as being at odds with the fatalistic and deterministic demands of tragedy.

While some critics and playwrights see the prevalent pessimism as an obstacle to the creation of tragedy and the presentation on the stage of a viable heroism, others, for instance Nietzsche, see optimism as the culprit. For example, George Steiner believes that it was the overbearing optimism and rational temper of the age that destroyed the tragic vision. He points out in *The Death of Tragedy* (1961) that eighteenth-century democratization, social optimism and rationalism contributed to the demise of tragedy, a genre grounded in catastrophe and dependent upon dark mystery. Unlike Krutch, Steiner sees irrationality – which he, like Krutch, associates with tragedy – as a dark and mysterious force that haunts humanity and is defeated during the Age of Reason. The Rousseauist belief in human perfectability and in social institutions, as well as the growing emphasis on social reform as the answer to suffering, mark the death of tragedy.

Steiner's historical examination of the origins of the liberal ideology in the eighteenth century and its effect on tragedy raises an important question: is it possible to write liberal tragedy? Or, in other words, is a democratic, reform-oriented, rationalistic belief system compatible with the fatalistic vision tragedy presumably requires and the heroic grandeur it demands of its protagonist? According to Steiner and many other critics,

> where the causes of disaster are temporal, where the conflict can be resolved through technical or social means we may have serious drama, but not tragedy. More pliant divorce laws could not alter the fate of Agamemnon; social psychiatry is no answer to Oedipus. But saner economic relations or better plumbing *can* resolve the grave crises in the dramas of Ibsen. (8)

It has become a critical truism that the tragic view is incompatible with social ameliorism. Tragedy, unlike social drama, deals with the eternal problems of humanity, it is said. One response to this apparent irreconcilability of tragedy and social drama (or other forms of realism) is to discard tragedy as no longer viable; the other is to write essentially non-contemporary, traditional plays; the third, it seems, is to attempt to reconcile tragedy and realism in order to create a specifically modern version of tragedy.

The question of what constitutes a fertile ground for tragedy has fuelled a continuing debate. Gassner's 'traditionalists' argue that the existence of tragedy is dependent, among other factors, upon a shared understanding of established morals and customs. They look to the Elizabethan and Jacobean ages as examples of societies with stable beliefs and shared value systems. Their insistence on social and political stability and on a unified value system as necessary prerequisites bespeaks an inflexible definition of tragedy, often accompanied by an uncritical adherence to the Aristotelian canon and to its use for judging all dramatic tragedies, regardless of the historical and aesthetic context. It does not account for the necessary transformations any genre may undergo.

There are also those who believe that it is in fact the transitional historical period that is the most likely setting for tragedy. In 'Tragedy as a Dramatic Art', Hegel states that tragedy is inherent in the historical process and therefore most vibrant during transitional periods. The requisite for tragic action is the heroic world condition, the presence of heroic times 'when the universal ethical forces have neither acquired the independent stability of definite political legislation or moral commands and obligations' (Paolucci and Paolucci, 63). It is in these times that a collision between two mutually exclusive ethical imperatives occurs, stimulating action on the part of the tragic hero. This collision, arising in an act of violation of the status quo, is 'a change in the previously existent condition of harmony, a change which is still in process' (Paolucci and Paolucci 113). According to this definition, tragedy is a dialectical working out of the conflict between two irreconcilable ethical forces.

Nietzsche believes that tragedy is born at times of a weakened hold of the scientific spirit on the world and asserts in *The Birth of Tragedy* that:

> The fact that the dialectical drive toward knowledge and scientific optimism has succeeded in turning tragedy from its course suggests that there may be an eternal conflict between the theoretical and tragic world view, in which case tragedy could be reborn only when science had at last pushed to its limits and, faced with those limits, been forced to renounce its claim to universal validity. (104)

Seeing the conflict between the metaphysical and the scientific outlook as a recurring one, he speaks not only of the origins of classical tragedy but also of the possible re-emergence of a tragic era in his own time. He believes that the prevalent optimism of the age has finally come under attack and that the growing dissatisfaction with Socratic culture will result in the gradual reawakening of the Dionysiac spirit.

Furthermore, he speaks of modern man as 'stripped of myth, [standing] . . . famished among all his pasts and . . . [digging] frantically for roots, be it among the most remote antiquities' (137). O'Neill echoes Nietzsche when he refers to the modern playwright's need to

> dig at the roots of the sickness of today as he feels it – the death of the old God and the failure of science and materialism to give any satisfying new one for the surviving primitive religious instinct to find a meaning for life in, and to comfort its fears of death with. (*Nine Plays*, xvii)

The playwright believes that this search for a new 'god' must be at the centre of any modern literary work aspiring to greatness:

> It seems to me that anyone trying to do big work nowadays must have this big subject behind all the little subjects of his plays or novels, or he is simply scribbling around the surface of things and has no more status than a parlor entertainer. (xvii)

According to O'Neill, the theatre, for both the spectator and the playwright, provides a means of dramatizing the Nietzschean myth of mythless humanity.

Almost a hundred years after Nietzsche wrote *The Birth of Tragedy*, Albert Camus, in his lecture 'On the Future of Tragedy' (1955), placed modern civilization on the threshold of a potentially tragic era. The present age, Camus asserts, is characterized by both rationalism and excessiveness, by a tension which lends itself to tragic interpretation. Tragedy by definition deals with irreconcilable tension; it exists between 'the poles of extreme nihilism and unlimited hope' (304), between reason and mystery. An overwhelming 'inner anguish' characterizes modern life, he says; the question is whether it will find tragic expression. Camus argues in his lecture that due to historical pressures, the great era of hope, progress and individualism is coming to an end as 'little by little the individual is recognizing his limits' (306). The humanism of the enlightenment has culminated in an era which has lost respect for humanity; therefore, '[the] world that the eighteenth-century individual thought he could conquer and transform by reason and science has in fact taken shape, but it's a monstrous one' (306). The faith and self-confidence that Nietzsche found so oppressively optimistic have all but eroded, and a new sense of fate – historical determinism – has emerged, as, paradoxically, 'humanity has refashioned a hostile destiny with the very weapons it used to reject fatality' (306).

It suffices to examine Krutch's preoccupation with tragedy to see that it is born of a conflict between the scientific, materialistic and rationalistic world-view dominating modern life and the idealistic and mythic world-view he wishes to maintain or reintroduce. And it is the awareness of this same tension that has prompted some playwrights to turn to tragedy. Anderson, Miller and Williams – who do not concern themselves directly with 'the death of the old God', but who also explore the 'sickness of today' – see the modern malaise as a function of a loss of idealism, the latter viewed from a different perspective in each case. As a result, their interest in tragedy is triggered not only by their disillusionment with the materialism and rationalism (!) of American society, but also by their firm belief in human potential and in the necessity of faith. The realities of living in an overwhelmingly despairing world inspire them to dramatize the endurance of idealism. In an age when humanity's insignificance and lack of control are being constantly lamented, it is no wonder that playwrights should place such a premium on the protagonists' reshaping of their destinies and that this should be an important criterion of heroism. The strength of uncompromising convictions and the determination to act upon them endow the protagonists with heroic dimensions. Having established this, however, the modern dramatist is still faced with the task of identifying causes worthy of such heroism. Repeatedly, in the plays of Anderson, Miller and Williams, worthy cause has to do with the preservation of individual moral integrity in a world of disintegrating values and moral relativism.

The tragedies these playwrights attempt to write between the wars and after the Second World War show the protagonists searching for meaning and attempting to gain some control over their own existence in a universe that has become increasingly hostile to their needs. Caught between the overhelming materialism of the age and their own idealistic impulse, the playwrights dramatize the unresolved tension between the rationalistic/materialistic world-view and the tragic/idealistic vision. They portray the heroism of the idealist's quest in a utilitarian world, of the potentially tragic figure's struggle in a dehumanized universe, of the self-conscious protagonist's internalized battle between materialistic imperatives and idealistic impulses. Two approaches to crises, on the part of the protagonist, become apparent here: that of the survivor and that of the moral victor. The survivor figure appears in the guises of the materialist, the pragmatist, the conformist, the cynic, the stronger and the predator. The moral victor – the emblem of heroism in all these plays – is invariably the idealist, the romantic, the non-conformist, the victim, the outsider.

Defining the situation in various ways and using different approaches, the playwrights dramatize the protagonists' struggle to combat alienation and counter meaninglessness. They take the view that to reinstate faith, they must begin with individuals and chronicle their attempt to define themselves. In many of these plays the conflict is not so much between a 'theoretical' and a 'tragic' world view, but rather between a world-view engendered by a utilitarian, faithless, materialistic world of power and a view championed and defended by the opposing force – usually the individual – representing faith and idealism.

Miller asserts in his essay 'The Family in Modern Drama' that

> all plays we call great, let alone those we call serious, are ultimately involved with some aspect of a single problem. It is this: How may a man make of the outside world a home? How and in what ways must he struggle, what must he strive to change and overcome within himself and outside himself if he is to find safety, the surroundings of love, the ease of soul, the sense of identity and honor which, evidently, all men have connected in their memories with the idea of family? (73)

Although Miller's focus here seems to be exclusively the familial domain, the search for a home can be seen in a wider sense as a quest for a place within society, and even beyond that, as an existential search for meaning. Certainly the preoccupation with finding a 'home' or a place of refuge from the hostile world figures in such diverse plays as *Death of a Salesman, A Streetcar Named Desire* and *Long Day's Journey into Night*, among others.

This quest for a home is often closely tied to a flight from a past action; the anguished protagonists are haunted by transgressions and seek oblivion in a safe haven. Such is the fate of Willy Loman and Blanche DuBois, for instance. As Linda Loman tells us, Willy's quest for relevance takes the form of 'a little boat looking for a harbor' (76). In a similar search for solace, Blanche is driven from one man to another 'hunting for some protection' (146). For her, Mitch is 'a cleft in the rock of the world' (147), a place to hide. At the same time, Willy and Blanche yearn for the past which was a period of innocence and which they are no longer able to recapture. Thus, both the fear of the past and a yearning for it characterize the hero's or heroine's plight. This duality forms the central theme in such diverse plays as *The Glass Menagerie, A Streetcar Named Desire* and *Death of a Salesman.*

In 'The Family in Modern Drama' Miller maintains that great plays such as *Hamlet, Lear* or *Oedipus*

> are all examining the concept of loss, of man's deprivation of a once-extant state of bliss unjustly shattered – a bliss, a state of equilibrium . . . It is as though both playwright and audience believed that they had once had an identity, a *being*, somewhere

> in the past which in the present has lost its completeness, its definitiveness, so that the central force making for pathos in these large and thrusting plays is the paradox which Time bequeaths to us all: we cannot go home again, and the world we live in is an alien place. (74–5)

The sense of alienation – from one's society, family and finally oneself – is germane to several of Miller's plays and is usually described in terms of the complex relationship between past and present. For instance, in the course of *Death of a Salesman* Willy becomes alienated from the present; at the same time, he mentally and emotionally submerges himself in the very past he is trying desperately to both understand and escape. Miller has said that 'in his desperation to justify his life, Willy Loman has destroyed the boundaries between now and then' ('Introduction to the Collected Plays' 26). In other words, in order to reconcile himself to his past and make the present bearable, he enters the timeless world of subjective reality where he can feel at home.

Unlike Miller, Anderson resorts to the historical past in order to elevate drama: he writes history plays in a nostalgic attempt to recreate traditional tragedy. He chooses to set his tragedies in the distant past because, as he says in 'A Prelude to Poetry in the Theatre',

> poetic tragedy had never been successfully written about its own place and time. There is not one tragedy by Aeschylus, Sophocles, Euripides, Shakespeare, Corneille or Racine which did not have the advantage of a setting either far away or long ago. (37–8)

His attempt to bring uplifting spiritual transformation to the modern stage begins with his turning to the past, to verse drama and to aristocratic tragedy, because he believes that:

> A great play cannot deal with ordinary people speaking commonplaces. It cannot deal with ordinary life. It has to concern itself with definitely unusual individuals in unusual situations, lifted by extraordinary emotions to extraordinary actions. (*Dramatist in America*, 19–20.)

Unable to find in the modern democratic era these conditions for tragedy, he turns to pre-collectivist times for his heroes and heroines and relies on the historical setting to endow his protagonist with significance.

In such early plays as *The Masque of Kings, Second Overture* and *Elizabeth the Queen* he shows the endurance of idealism in the face of the corrupting influence of power and writes about idealism and revolution from the perspective of a world that has lost faith in all causes. The only cause left in such a world is moral self-preservation through physical self-destruction. It is not just the corruption of power that Anderson dramatizes but, more fundamentally, the insidiousness of political power *per se* and the heroism of the person who chooses individual integrity and love over power. He imposes his liberal democratic humanism on the historical material and thus circumvents the specific technical problems associated with writing modern tragedy. The figures he chooses to dramatize in the later plays – Jesus, Joan of Arc, Socrates – function as exempla of the struggle for freedom and of the affirmation of faith in liberal individualism.

In *Elizabeth the Queen* (1929)[1] the nature of political power and the internal turmoil of the wielders and would-be wielders of it are examined. The play centres on the conflict – both romantic and political – between Elizabeth and Essex, between power and love. The collision has its external and its internal manifestation: the power struggle is complicated by the love interest, the love interest by the power struggle; power and love vie for primacy within each of the characters. In the context of the play, power is an aphrodisiac and yet, as Elizabeth discovers, is meaningless without love. This simultaneous interdependence and exclusiveness of characters and concepts must necessarily have its tragic implications.

Elizabeth vacillates but at the critical moment chooses power over love. Of course, historically speaking, she could not have chosen differently given the political contingencies; nonetheless, her choice is condemned by Anderson who transforms the historical material into a democratic statement against power and political ambitions when he ignores Renaissance attitudes to power and politics. Here, history is not the context in which the characters act but rather a decorative, potentially heroic backdrop against which they voice their liberal-democratic concerns. Paradoxically, Anderson relies on the depiction of a heroic age and on echoes of Shakespeare to provide the grandeur and to remedy the diminution of the hero that is concomitant with democracy and mass individualism; yet he uses the setting against itself when he rejects everything it implies. He chooses to deal with a past when one could presumably speak of order and of ultimate victory in another world and thus endow his protagonist's sacrifice – which in the modern context is limited to the individualistic assertion 'in myself I know'[2] – with considerable significance.

Historical considerations and concerns with theatrical splendour require that Elizabeth be in the foreground; although she does loom large over the action of the play, it is Essex whose downfall follows the tragic pattern. He is driven by conflicting ambitions; he recognizes the irreconcilable tension inherent in his desires; he chooses honorable death over an ignominious political life. In his initial drive for political power Essex sins not against a moral order or even against an established socio-political order but against his own moral integrity. The individual's sense of identity is Anderson's focus here and in his other plays. The dramatic and ideological implications of Essex's acceptance of the death sentence are blurred by historical considerations which necessarily determine the tone of the play and preclude a thorough examination of the characters' motives. Nonetheless, Essex's behaviour places him in a class with Anderson's early defeatist heroes who react to evil rather than act against it. These figures choose not to participate in life for fear of losing integrity. Their suicidal tendencies bring to mind some of the protagonists of Miller's early plays – for instance Joe Keller and Willy Loman – who kill themselves to preserve their integrity. Anderson has said that 'the theme of tragedy has always been victory in defeat, a man's conquest of himself, in the face of annihilation' ('Yes, By the Eternal', 51). Essex accepts death rather than compromise his ideals and cooperate with evil or allow his own potential evil to dominate. Willy Loman and Joe Keller commit suicide because they realize that their whole life has been a compromise dedicated to materialism and to power, and they refuse to continue living the lie. Their actions – like Essex's – exemplify the modern concern with individual integrity and the skepticism concerning power.

In *The Masque of Kings* (1937), a play set during the twilight of the Austro-Hungarian monarchy, Anderson places the corruption of idealism into the context of historical change and revolution. The idealistic and politically naïve crown prince Rudolph represents the advent of a liberal humanist era that promises to put an end to the royal masquerade. However, he also embodies Anderson's skepticism regarding social/political change and revolution.

Rudolph struggles with the paradox that power is needed to bring about justice but power corrupts and is inimical to justice; however, he falls victim to the fallacy of the political reformer who believes that it is possible to be both 'king' and 'man', to wrest power from the exploiters and use it for the good of the exploited without loss of justice or freedom. He is confronted with the irreconcilable conflict between introducing reforms, which may result in new injustices and in the eventual loss of freedom, and the exercise of traditional authority. As he gains power and gradually begins using dictatorial expedients, he realizes that he has become 'the thing I hate' and he has his moment of spiritual enlightenment, of Andersonian 'recognition':

> I see in one blinding light that he who
> thinks of justice cannot reach
> or hold power over men, that he who thinks
> of power, must whip his justice and his mercy
> close to heel.
>
> (137)

The impact of this irreconcilable conflict between justice and power, together with his lover's suicide, prompts him to kill himself.

Before he does that, he paints a dark picture of the moribund monarchy and prophesies revolution:

> Now the earth boils up again and the new men
> and nations rise in fire
> to fall in rock, and there shall be new kings,
> . . . a new batch of devil-faces, ikons
> made of men's hope of liberty, all worshipped
> as bringers of the light, but conquerors,
> like those we follow.
>
> (137)

Through Rudolph, the playwright reasons from the fact of short-lived idealism to the futility of revolution and to a glorification of defeatism. Rudolph is an ineffectual idealist who expatiates – with echoes of Ecclesiastes – on the vanity of political reform in the face of the cyclical nature of history. With new revolutions come

> the new sowers of death – fools like myself
> who rush themselves to power to set men free
> and hold themselves in power by killing men,
> as time was, as time will be, time out of mind
> unto this last, forever.
> (137)

Like Essex, Rudolph dies for love rather than face his own corruption.

Second Overture (1938), a one-act play on the aftermath of the Russian Revolution, illustrates Anderson's attitude to political idealism and heroism. Gregor the revolutionary disassociates himself from the post-revolutionary reign of terror – the second overture of the title – and heroically accepts the counterrevolutionary's death sentence as he exclaims: 'Better to lose than to lose your faith' (170). Gregor is placed in a position where he must accept the tenets and methods of the new regime, although they go against everything he had in his idealism fought for in the revolution. Failing this, he must face death. To Anderson the choice is clear and tragic in its implication.

During the war years Anderson saw the need to transcend the defeatism he dramatized in his early plays and addressed himself directly to the modern crisis of faith and to the need to break out of the impasse. His contemporary play *Key Largo* (1939) dramatizes the process of becoming a victor, not just a victim of circumstances, and explores its tragic inevitability. In the Prologue to the play Anderson sets up the central opposition between victor and survivor, between idealism and pragmatism (or cynicism, he believes) as he shows Americans in the Spanish Civil War questioning the cause. Victor, the realistic idealist, analyses the fight for freedom:

> Hasn't it always looked the same, the fight for
> freedom? It's never respectable. It's led by
> unscrupulous fanatics, each eyeing the others'
> throats. They're followed by a rabble that pulls
> down all the walls and lets the roofs fall in
> on them. A lot of people die, good and bad, but
> there is more freedom later, for the next
> generation, there is. If you want a clean,
> Armageddon battle, all the beasts of hell against

the angels of light, you won't get that,
not in this world. (10–11)

Victor's vision of history and of revolution is no less bleak than Rudolph's. Nonetheless, he has not lost his faith and is willing to die for his beliefs in a world bereft of belief. He embodies the never-dying optimism, the faith in a better future built upon a clear understanding of all-pervasive uncertainty, evil and pessimism.

When King McCloud, at this point in the play a pessimistic materialist and coward, asks Victor why should he go on, why risk death, Victor answers: 'Because there is no God'. The materialist's evidence is the idealistic Victor's justification for struggle:

Because the sky's quite empty,
just as you said. The scientists have been over it
with a fine-tooth comb and a telescope, and the verdict
is, no God, nothing there, empty and sterilized,
like a boiled test-tube. But if there's no God there
and nothing inside me I have any respect for
then I'm done. Then I don't live, and I couldn't.
So I stay here to keep whatever it is
alive that's alive inside me.
(20)

Victor feels the need to create his own faith for fear of spiritual death. King McCloud, on the other hand, deserts the battlefield. Later, haunted by his act of betrayal, he seeks out Victor's family in Florida and assuming the identity of his dead friend, accepts responsibility for Victor's past actions. His sacrificial act is one of expiation for the sin of betrayal of friends, country, ideals and ultimately oneself.

It is Victor's blind father d'Alcala who makes King see that he had suffered a spiritual death in Spain. The blind seer (Esdras in *Winterset* and d'Alcala in *Key Largo*), who speaks of the need to go forward with determination in spite of uncertainty, best exemplifies Anderson's brand of optimism. D'Alcala delivers the Andersonian message:

that's our challenge—
to find ourselves in this desert of dead light-years,
blind, all of us, in a kingdom of the blind,

> living by appetite in a fragile shell
> of dust and water; yet to take this dust
> and water and our range of appetites
> and build them toward some vision of a god
> of beauty and unselfishness and truth.
> (11)

Anderson plants his faith in the soil of despair – a paradox which becomes the crux of his, and also other playwrights', tragic vision.

Miller has also been intent upon dramatizing the idealist's striving to preserve faith – that is, the belief in ethical and social responsibility and the moral strength to uphold it – in the midst of faithlessness. A morally possessed man's quest for the truth and his fight against spiritual death are at the centre of Miller's melodramatic thesis play *All My Sons* (1947). Miller has said in 'Morality and Modern Drama' that the play 'is not so much an attack but an exposition, so to speak, of the want of value' (195). It is the catastrophe-laden story of a man who plays an important role in society (he manufactures airplane parts) but who does not think beyond the familial domain or beyond the profit motive. He acts irresponsibly; during World War Two he ships out defective parts in order to meet the deadline and to make the necessary profit. In the process he unwittingly causes the death of a number of young soldiers, including that of his son. He escapes punishment, but the past comes to haunt him in the present in the form of his other son, an unrelenting idealist who drives him to admit his guilt and ultimately forces him to come face to face with himself.

The play dramatizes the conflict between Chris, the champion of brotherly love and social responsibility, and the father Joe Keller, spokesman for the business ethic and for asocial individualism. Chris (much like King McCloud in *Key Largo*) carries the terrible burden of survivor's guilt. He has come out of the war alive, though by no means unscathed: he realizes that the idealists died in the war, and the practical ones survived. And it is during the war that he comes to value brotherly responsibility. He is not comfortable with the post-war situation, with the callous continuation of life. More importantly, he feels that his father's business capitalized on the deaths of the soldiers, including that of his brother. His unrelenting quest for the truth concerning his father's crime is an expiation of sorts for his own stultifying sense of guilt. Chris' final moral victory resides in driving his father to pay the wages of sin, to commit suicide. Through an uncompromising dedication to an ideal and its enforcement at all costs, Chris escapes his spiritual death and in the process causes his father's physical death.

Two types of idealism clash in the play: Chris' self-righteous search for the truth and Joe's total dedication to his business and his faith in the primacy of the profit motive. Although the audience is asked to share Chris' ideas – he is the most eloquent figure and delivers the key lines – their sympathies must necessarily be divided. Presumably, they are victims of the very same propaganda, products of the same ideological machine, as Joe Keller is. His systematic destruction by an avenging son must strike a sympathetic chord. And yet, the audience must also side with Chris who, despite his unforgiving nature, is identified, through a number of references in the play, as a Christ figure.

Miller describes the father, Joe Keller, as an ordinary man, an 'uneducated man for whom there is still wonder in many commonly known things, a man whose judgment must be dredged out of experience and a peasant-like common sense' (59). Desperately clinging to his image of himself as a father, Joe Keller puts all his faith into his relationship with his son when he exclaims: 'My only accomplishment is my son. I ain't brainy. That's all I accomplished' (97). And later, in Act Three, he utters the ominous lines: 'I'm his father and he's my son, and if there's something bigger than that I'll put a bullet in my head!' (120). As Joe's crime comes to light in the course of the play, he attempts to convince Chris that he did it all for business and therefore for the good of the family.

Chris, the voice of the community's conscience, is outraged by his father's limited and callous view:

> I was dying every day and you were killing my boys and you did it for me? . . . Is that as far as your mind can see, the business? What the hell do you mean, you did it for me? Don't you have a country? don't you live in the world? What the hell are you? You're not even an animal, no animal kills his own, what are you? What must I do to you? I ought to tear the tongue out of your mouth, what must I do? (116)

Chris' act of unmasking has a high price: he loses his father as well as all illusions concerning him. Although he has in some way rectified the wrong and thus regained his faith in justice, his pursuit of the truth has brought him face to face with a painful revelation.

Not only has he chosen truth at all cost, he has betrayed his father who had previously betrayed Chris' brother.

Joe Keller's suicide is a response not only to a guilty conscience but also to a profound disillusionment. Through his total dedication to material concerns, apparently for the sake of his family, Keller is alienated from the society he is presumably meant to serve through his business. Ultimately he becomes alienated from his family and disillusioned with everything he had valued. Miller states in the 'Introduction to the Collected Plays' that the play examines the roots of that alienation:

> The fortress which *All My Sons* lays siege to is the fortress of unrelatedness. It is an assertion not so much of a morality of right and wrong, but of a moral world's being such because men cannot walk away from certain of their deeds. (19)

In other words, because Joe Keller is alienated from his society, as a result of his egoistic pursuit of material wealth, he is unable to see that he must bear certain social responsibilities.

Miller believes that Joe Keller's asocial behaviour is dangerous; *All My Sons* is a social play because it warns against this danger. It is not the legal and moral judgement that comes down on the manufacturer that is the central concern in the play, Miller claims, because

> [the play's] 'socialness' does not reside in its having dealt with the crime of selling defective materials to a nation at war . . . It is that the crime is seen as having roots in a certain relationship of the individual to society, and to a certain indoctrination he embodies, which, if dominant, can mean a jungle existence for all of us. (19)

All My Sons attempts to expose Keller's social irresponsibility and, like *Death of a Salesman,* to offer the motivation of love as an alternative to the motivation of material success. In both plays, the son represents this saner alternative which the father ignores all his life, the difference being that whereas in the earlier play love is understood in terms of brotherhood and social consciousness, in the later play it is seen in terms of familial and conjugal love. It is Joe's unquestioning conformity to the prevalent anti-social ethic that destroys him. He is a prototype of the Miller character who is intensely dedicated to a false ideal, usually to the most alienating and destructive aspect of the popular social ethos. As Miller points out, Joe Keller's problem is not one of not knowing right from wrong but has to do with the fact 'that his cast of mind cannot admit that he, personally, has any viable connection with his world, his universe, or his society' (19).

Following mutual betrayals, both father and son come to a recognition the impact of which is tragic. According to Miller,

> at a certain point, one learns something which is true, profound, and which the person cannot support. There is illumination that kills. That's where we get into an area called tragedy. (Evans, 76–7)

It is the intensity of this illumination and of its final effect, as much as the heroic intensity of the protagonist's quest, that provides the tragic dimension. Society is a powerful image-maker, and what Miller calls 'conformity to a perverse image' (Centola, 345–60) can have catastrophic consequences. The conformist who accepts societal values is as vulnerable as the non-conformist. In fact, the destruction of 'consenting victims' (Corrigan, *Arthur Miller*, 131–42), as Gerald Weales calls them, best exemplifies the tragedy of a whole society not just of the isolated individual. In some of Miller's plays it is precisely the conformist, the person who has appropriated the societal lie, but whom that society has in the meantime betrayed, who suffers and who is crushed by the system.

Joe Keller is a well-adjusted and highly successful member of society who does not question his own actions until he is forced to accept their consequences. On the other hand, Willy Loman is only an unsuccessful, would-be Joe Keller who is sacrificed to his self-delusion, lack of judgement, incompetence and illusions concerning the false values of the system. Although Willy may protest against the system, he is in fact deeply involved in it and suffers from his failure to become an integral part of it. Willy accepts society's rules (or at least his own interpretation of them) but is unwilling to accept its judgement. The house he inhabits is *'a dream rising out of reality'* (Act One, stage direction), and Willy cannot face that reality, much less its implications. When the system alienates him by showing him that he is no longer needed, he desperately tries to reintegrate.

If Keller represents the tragedy of success without ethical responsibility, Loman personifies the tragedy of failure in a success-oriented environment. Despite being a salesman, Willy does not understand, as Charley points out, that the 'only thing you got in this world is what you can sell' (192). His sentimental and naïve attachment to an older, presumably more humane, version of the 'American Dream' has no place in the modern pragmatic world of business into which he so desperately wishes to fit. Two conflicting desires motivate him: first, the yearning for an innocent rural America of the past where, he firmly believes, 'personality' rather than profit defined a man's worth; and second, the need to be successful in the modern world of business. The former, if it ever existed, is no longer conceivable; the latter will be his demise.

Willy's tragic mistake, according to Miller, is that he breaks the unwritten but very powerful 'law of success', which declares 'that a failure in society and in business has no right to live'. This is a rather dubious law, Miller explains:

> Willy's law – the belief, in other words, which administers guilt to him – is not a civilizing statute whose destruction menaces us all; it is, rather, a deeply believed and deeply suspected 'good' which, when questioned as to its value, as it is in this play, serves more to raise our anxieties than to reassure us of the existence of an unseen but metaphysical system in the world. ('Introduction to the Collected Plays', 35)

As Miller explains, the law of success and its conflict with the opposing law of love form the central concern in the play. His attempt in the play is

> to counter this anxiety with an opposing system which, so to speak, is in race for Willy's faith, and it is the system of love which is the opposite of the law of success. It is embodied in Biff Loman, but by the time Willy can perceive his love it can serve only as an ironic comment upon the life he sacrificed for power and for success and its tokens. ('Introduction to the Collected Plays', 36)

Clearly, Miller's delineation of the dramatic conflict between power and love, or between materialism and idealism, has more in common with O'Neill's, Anderson's or Williams' treatment of the same subject than the discussions about his critique of capitalism would lead one to believe.

As the play opens, we see Willy in the final stages of his losing battle. Returning exhausted from yet another unaccomplished business trip, he has already lost grip on external reality. Unlike Quentin in *After the Fall,* who engages in highly analytical, conscious deliberation which constitutes the action of the play, Willy is controlled by his dreams and past experiences. We are told and shown that he is alienated from his work and from his sons; by being a prisoner to internal conflicts of his own, he is also alienated from the external reality which in this play constitutes part of the action. According to Miller, he

> is literally at that terrible moment when the voice of the past is no longer distant but quite as loud as the voice of the present. In dramatic terms the form therefore is this process, instead of being a once-removed summation or indication of it. ('Introduction to the Collected Plays', 26)

In wider terms, Willy's condition represents not just the wanderings of a mind that has lost its grip on reality, but also the painful attempt to recapture a past long gone by re-living it in the present. To a large extent, the intensity of the play, its effectiveness as theatre, is provided not by the action on the part of the protagonist, nor by his potentially heroic qualities, but by a sharp conflict between two levels of reality operating in the play: Willy's thought processes and hallucinations and the action occurring around him. The play's emotional power resides in this technical interplay between realism (the objective action of the present) and expressionism (Willy's subjective recollections). During the course of the play, past and present become increasingly meshed as Willy's wanderings seem to exist outside time. As the transparent set indicates, all physical and spatial barriers have been broken down; Willy essentially occupies the world inside his head,[3] where characters can move through walls and through time. He exists unconstrained in the past as well as in the present, ostensibly not unlike Tom Wingfield, the narrator of *The Glass Menagerie,* who moves freely into and out of the action as he takes up his role as one of the characters. Both he and Tom exist outside time; however, while Tom controls time, Willy is controlled and mastered by it.

In Act Two Willy is less and less able to deal with the present. He retreats deeper into the past and is completely overwhelmed by it. He finally understands that it was Biff's discovery of his adulterous act that drove father and son apart. His sudden realization that he had betrayed his son drives him to his death, for which he had been preparing from the beginning of the play. Although Miller has said that Willy's suicide is in repentance for the immoral adherence to false values, at the end Miller places strong emphasis on the issue of adultery. In fact, it is this act of Willy's that has presumably 'ruined' Biff's life and has been lying heavily on Willy's conscience. Like Lear, Willy comes to the realization that he was loved by his child; unlike Lear, he has gained no real understanding concerning his fate, let alone knowledge about the human condition.

Although Willy has gained no significant insight into his situation and still adamantly clings to his old values, this is not to say that he is unaware of his situation or that he is entirely unenlightened. As Miller suggests, Willy lives with an acute awareness of his alienation and of the emptiness of his life:

> Had Willy been unaware of his separation from values that endure he would have died contentedly while polishing his car probably on a Sunday afternoon with the ball game coming over the radio. But he was agonized by his awareness of being in a false position, so constantly haunted by the hollowness of all he had placed his faith in, so aware, in short, that he must somehow be filled in his spirit or fly apart, that he staked his very life on the ultimate assertion. That he had not the intellectual fluency to verbalize his situation is not the same thing as saying he lacked awareness, even an overly intensified consciousness that the life he had made was without form and inner meaning. ('Introduction to the Collected Plays', 34–5)

One must add that had Willy 'died contentedly while polishing his car', we would have not only a different Willy but also a very different play. For Miller, a small man's appropriately small and private protest which does little to disturb the order or even assault the environment becomes triumphant in its aspiration and intensity. Willy may have learned little in the course of the play about the system and his relationship to it; however, through his anguish and after his final act of salesmanship, the audience experiences an insight that is denied Willy.

At the end of the play, Willy's spiritual victory over himself resides in his recognition that his son loves him and has forgiven him. According to Miller, he is given his identity at the end – he reclaims his fatherhood. However, that

> he is unable to take this victory thoroughly to his heart, that it closes the circle for him and propels him to his death, is the wage of his sin, which was to have committed himself so completely to the counterfeits of dignity and the false coinage embodied in his idea of success that he can prove his existence only by bestowing 'power' on his posterity, a power deriving from the sale of his last asset, himself, for the price of his insurance policy. ('Introduction to the Collected Plays', 34)

It is significant that Miller refers to Willy's lifelong dedication to success as a 'sin'; in light of this, the ambivalence of Willy's suicide is especially important. While it is, in some sense, a heroic act of defiance in answer to the system's betrayal of the individual, it is also Willy's only 'successful' act of salesmanship. At the same time, it is his punishment for a crime, an act of penance for his sins. Willy makes the final decision to kill himself when he succumbs to his brother Ben's seductive voice of success, which is also the voice of death.

It is useful to compare the play with *A Streetcar Named Desire* in terms of the two plays' series of polarities: past/present, subjectivity/objectivity, illusion/reality, spiritual values/material values. Both Willy and Blanche cling to a past which cannot be recaptured, except in their imaginations, and perhaps never even existed. A faith in that past, a supposedly more humane and civilized period of American life, provides emotional sustenance and integrity. When illusions concerning the past are shattered – usually by another character whose interest it is to unmask the hero or heroine – the protagonist is destroyed as well: Blanche retreats into madness; Willy kills himself.

The past offers a haven to the troubled souls, but it is not as unblemished as they would like to believe. It harbors images of betrayal: Willy's adultery, Blanche's turning away from her homosexual husband. Haunted and paralyzed by guilt, Willy and Blanche are caught between a past of unspoken complexities and an unbearable present. Fugitives from a past which is in part a product of their idealistic imagination, they are in the end mercilessly destroyed by a present which offers neither understanding nor solace to their conscience-ridden souls.

To adjust to the present, self-betrayal is necessary; that is, one's integrity must be forsaken. The 'stable' characters in *Death of a Salesman* (Linda and Charley, for example) do not question the system; they try to make the best of the situation. Linda sacrifices all in her support of Willy, but in fact she does not really understand him. Stella Kowalski in *A Streetcar Named Desire* has adopted a pose of equilibrium – she has 'that almost narcotized tranquility that is in the faces of Eastern idols' (70) – and has accepted her fate, learned to tolerate Stanley's brutality.

Blanche, on the other hand, tries desperately to avoid the harsh light of reality, to protect her 'delicate beauty', for there is '*something about her uncertain manner as well as her white clothes, that suggests a moth*' (5). She comments that she 'can't stand a naked light bulb, any more than . . . a rude remark or a vulgar action' (60), and she hides in the shade of the paper lantern. In Scene Six, where she tells Mitch of her betrayal of Alan Grey, she describes her first discovery of love as the sudden turning on of 'a blinding light on something that had always been half in shadow' (114). When she had betrayed her husband, the light went off for ever: 'And then the searchlight which had been turned on the world was turned off again and never for one moment since has there been any light that's stronger than this-kitchen-candle'(115). Since then, Blanche has been unable to face the light; however, she is acutely aware of her fear of the truth when she exclaims:

> I don't want realism. I want magic! Yes, yes, magic! I try to give that to people. I misrepresent things to them, I don't tell truth, I tell what *ought* to be truth. And if that is sinful, then let me be damned for it! – *Don't turn the light on!* (145)

In the end, Blanche's protective layers of illusion are stripped away by Stanley, just as Willy's dreams are shattered by Biff. Willy is a self-deluded dreamer who has brought up his sons to believe in his dream as well. When Biff finally faces his father at the end of the play, he accuses him of 'never [having] told the truth for ten minutes in this house' (216). He proceeds to deflate Willy's ego and to shatter the father's illusions about his sons.

It is a critical commonplace that *A Streetcar Named Desire* dramatizes a conflict of opposites. Elia Kazan comments in his 'Notebook for *A Streetcar Named Desire*' that the play

> is a message from the dark interior. This twisted pathetic, confused bit of light and culture puts out a cry. It is snuffed out by the crude forces of violence, insensibility and vulgarity which

> exist in our South – and this cry is the play. (Cole and Krich Chinoy, 365)

Kazan characterizes Blanche as 'a social type, an emblem of a dying civilization' and Stanley as the 'basic animal cynicism of today'. In a similar vein, John Gassner sees Blanche's fate as the 'tragedy of a fallen member of the Southern landed aristocracy' (*The Theatre in Our Times*, 357) who clings to her idea of herself as an exceptional individual.

Kazan, Gassner, and others as well, view Blanche as the product of a vanished world desperately clinging to tradition. They see her as the victim of the brutal Stanley, her demise as symptomatic of the destruction of a noble past by a crude, materialistic present. While this is certainly part of the truth, it is not an accurate description. To consider Blanche, as Kazan does, 'a butterfly in the jungle' and to reduce the play to a simple conflict between refinement and barbarism is tantamount to seeing Willy Loman as no more than a victim of capitalism. It is undeniable that Willy is a victim of capitalism and that Blanche is a victim of barbaric philistinism; however, the struggle of the protagonist against his or her immediate environment is an external manifestation of the internal struggle with a guilty conscience. Similarly, the external dualities are reflected in the protagonist's conflict-ridden inner world.

Not only do Blanche and Stanley represent the moral victor and the physical victor, the hunted and the hunter, refinement and barbarism, decadence and robustness, death and life, old and new, feminine and masculine, but Blanche herself – white as her name indicates and red as her robe suggests – embodies the dualities. She may be the moth destroyed by the harsh light, but she is also the tiger Stanley refers to in Scene Ten. It is her guilt regarding her husband's suicide, as much as the loss of the plantation Belle Reve and the dawning of a new era, that causes her alienation from the present. She atones for this guilt through her suffering at the hands of Stanley. While she voices her disgust concerning him, her attitude, like Williams', is in fact ambivalent: she is both repulsed and attracted; she is attracted because she is repulsed. Stanley, 'the gaudy seed bearer', 'a richly feathered male bird among hens' (24), is a caricature of the unspoiled Lawrentian natural man and represents the brutality of the present. Unlike the Lawrentian hero, however, Stanley is associated with business (it is often forgotten that he is a travelling salesman like Willy Loman) and with industry (his threatening presence is reinforced through the lights and the sounds of the locomotive) not only with free-spirited sexuality.

To Blanche, he is a prehistoric monster, the image of uncivilized man:

> He acts like an animal, has an animal's habits! Eats like one, moves like one, talks like one! There's even something – sub-human – something not quite to the stage of humanity yet! Yes, something – ape-like about him . . . Stanley Kowalski – survivor of the stone age! Bearing the raw meat home from the kill in the jungle! (83)

Blanche of course sees herself as cultured and morally superior. Like Anderson's visionaries and Williams' tortured heroines, she speaks of progress in an attempt to gain her sister's sympathy and turn her against Stanley:

> Maybe we are a long way from being made in God's image, but . . . there has been *some* progress since then! Such things as art – as poetry and music – such kinds of new light have come into the world since then! In some kinds of people some tenderer feelings have had some little beginning! That we have got to make *grow*! And *cling* to, and hold as our flag! In this dark march toward whatever it is we're approaching . . . *Don't – don't hang back with the brutes!* (83)

One cannot always take Blanche's histrionic outbursts seriously not only because her impassioned pleas often verge on the ridiculous and are reminiscent of Amanda Wingfield's (in *The Glass Menagerie*) pathetic recollections of her past, but also because in the figure of Blanche one glimpses the playwright's own ironic self-dramatization and in her battle with Stanley his own repulsion/attraction to a brutal, sexually raw, intellectually and culturally unsophisticated male figure. Although popular wisdom would have it that Blanche is objectified by Stanley (that is, turned into a sex object), Stanley, too, is an object for Blanche – both thing and objective. Blanche's response to Stanley is ambivalent. In her initial encounter with Stanley, Blanche sees that now that Belle Reve is nothing more than a 'bunch of old papers' in Stanley's 'big, capable hands' (44), he may be what the DuBois women need to mix with their blood (45) because he has vitality, virility and vulgar pragmatism – everything that Blanche's suffocating past lacks.

He takes special pride in having brought down Stella to his own level and reminds her of his triumph:

> When we first met, me and you, you thought I was common. How right you was, baby. I was common as dirt. You showed me the snapshot of the place with the columns. I pulled you down off them columns and how you loved it, having them colored lights going! And wasn't we happy together, wasn't it all okay till she showed here? (137)

Viewing Blanche as an unpleasant intruder and a threat to his marriage, he is determined to strip off her mask of respectability and refinement, to pull her down from the columns and to reveal the debased creature he believes her to be.

Blanche confides in Mitch that from the moment she saw Stanley, she realized that he would be her executioner. Knowing this, she provokes Stanley; she is drawn to her Nemesis in much the same way that the meek white character in Williams' homoerotic short story 'Desire and the Black Masseur' seeks out a masseur, a sadistic black cannibalist, who massages him with great force and finally devours him. When Stanley finds out about Blanche's past, he rapes her to demonstrate his mastery of her and his contempt for her. But in a sense his uncovering of her past, his shattering of all her illusions and his desecration, through the rape, of everything she represents exorcise her haunted past. Blanche is simultaneously unburdened and destroyed.

Willy, too, has an ambivalent attitude towards his 'executioners'. He is a 'consenting victim', but in fact he does not fully understand that to which he gave his consent. He conforms but does it so unsuccessfully – due partly to idealism, partly to incompetence – that he is destroyed. He sees no connection between his brother Ben's success and his own employer's attitude to business. He fails to comprehend that while he conforms, his value will be measured in terms of his usefulness. When he sees that he will be mercilessly discarded, he rebels. Just as Blanche, having lost the plantation as well as her reputation, refuses to forfeit her image of herself as a plantation belle and a woman of higher sensibilities, Willy continues to envision himself as a well-liked businessman even after he has failed. Because he insists on seeing and interpreting the world in his own way, he partakes of that heroic idealism which Miller describes as 'the fanatic insistence upon his self-conceived role' ('Introduction to the Collected Plays', 33). One could argue that in Willy's case it might be more appropriate to speak of mock-heroic rather than heroic qualities. He does not fall in the course of the play; he is deflated. His bourgeois vision of grandeur is shattered by his son Biff who reminds him that Willy Loman is a dime a dozen. However, Willy's passionate struggle, in the last hours of his life, to justify the life of a salesman is heroic in its intensity and anguish, and tragic in its failure.

The main characters in *Death of a Salesman* and *A Streetcar Named Desire* may be misguided in their understanding of reality, but they strive for an authenticity and partake of an idealism entirely alien to the reality of the well-adjusted characters. Their limited heroism lies in their refusal, even at the cost of self-destruction, to accept with tranquility a role that the outside world would impose on them and in their inability to walk away from failure.

Key Largo, Death of a Salesman, All My Sons and *A Streetcar Named Desire* suggest, each in its own manner, that in a world of moral relativity, the recognition of a transgression is in itself evidence of moral fortitude. Not only the willingness to suffer for a belief but also the capacity for self-condemnation is the mark of heroism in these plays: King McCloud, Joe Keller, Blanche DuBois and others are not condemned by society for their acts; they are their own judges – albeit provoked by a destructive antagonist – and choose physical death over spiritual death. Inherent in their guilty flight from a past action, in their quest for understanding and their desire for judgement, is also the struggle against meaninglessness.

3

Martyrdom as Heroism

In *Key Largo, Death of a Salesman* and *A Streetcar Named Desire* the idealistic protagonists' conflicts with the materialistic society may end in their physical destruction, but they also signal their moral triumph. The protagonists are destroyed, and the audience is made to believe that they have been condemned by an environment that failed to conform to the moral standards set by the playwright through the protagonist. Theirs is a struggle against a valueless world and against a cynical majority (often embodied in the protagonist figure) bent upon alienating or destroying the outsider; the protagonists' victories most often reside in the preservation of personal integrity and in the uncompromising adherence to an idealized vision of the world, even at the cost of self-destruction.

Death of a Salesman and *A Streetcar Named Desire* begin with the protagonist's movement toward death; however, they also indicate that this defeatist behaviour follows a time of disillusionment which was preceded by a long period of idealism. And it is this idealism – which in a revised form accompanies the protagonists even to their demise – that characterizes Willy's and Blanche's heroism. Willy dies happy in the thought that he has ensured Biff's future; Blanche can now depend on the kindness of strangers. In a sense, the self-destructiveness is a direct result of the idealism, for it is the total dedication to the ideal – however misguided and untenable; indeed, the less tenable, the more heroic it seems – that results in the disintegration of personality, alienation from the community and even death. This pattern, of course, presupposes a less than ideal social and moral order, one which although hostile (or worse – indifferent) to the protagonist's ideals, does not call for his or her sacrifice and, in fact, does not recognize it as such. Linda Loman's lack of understanding at the end of the 'Requiem' in *Death of a Salesman* is symptomatic of this general breakdown of communication between the self-destructive protagonist and his or her social and familial environment.

The idea of a corrupt society and a fallen humanity successfully accommodates the accompanying image of the special individual who willingly undergoes suffering for a cause. In an attempt to endow the victimized protagonist with dignity, perhaps even heroic grandeur, Anderson, Williams and Miller depict the protagonist's anguish and sacrifice in terms which resemble martyrdom; that is, they dramatize self-aware suffering and deliberate acts of passive resistance. One may find this approach to heroism not only in plays about actual martyrdom – for example, *The Crucible* or Anderson's *Joan of Lorraine* and *Journey to Jerusalem* – but also in those where the protagonists are perceived as martyrs by virtue of their dedication to an untenable ideal, alienation from the group and spiritual anguish, and where the society is shown to be morally blemished – for example in *Death of a Salesman* and *A Streetcar Named Desire.*

By emphasizing suffering for a cause and endowing modern characters with traits of the martyr, the dramatists confer upon their protagonists dignity and fill their actions with purpose. The alienated and victimized individual is shown, like the martyr, to be not only a stranger in a corrupt world but, more importantly, a morally superior being precisely by virtue of an estrangement from commonplace ethics. This view of heroism on one hand confirms the spiritual impoverishment lamented by some critics and playwrights and on the other belies the sense of historical discontinuity and existential absurdity through its dramatization of higher human potential.

Although a diminished world accommodates only diminished forms of martyrdom, martyrdom is a fitting metaphor for, if not a literal description of, the alienated outcast's abandonment or persecution by society as a result of his or her dedication to a cause. This need not be a social, political or ethical cause, or in fact anything we usually describe as a 'cause'; however, it must be a dedication to beliefs or feelings. Again, in this contemporary sense, the outcast has not been literally exiled from society the way a Lear has been; rather, his or her alienation is a perceived one, not a literal one, and is often self-imposed and thus inescapable.

The figure of the martyr is closely related to that of the anti-hero and the victim. Both, but especially the latter, are considered quintessentially modern heroes. Both, as well as the martyr, suffer at the hands of stronger, more powerful forces. However, what distinguishes the martyr from the anti-hero and the victim is an ethical awareness and a sense of purpose and direction: the victim and the anti-hero are simply unwilling objects of victimization who, even if able to articulate their suffering, have not willed the situation that brings about their destruction. Passive endurance is their sole accomplishment. Auden reminds us, in 'The Martyr as Dramatic Hero', that the martyr is a type of human sacrifice for the community, 'a man chosen by a social group to die to promote its spiritual and material welfare' (150). However, what distinguishes the martyr from the ordinary sacrificial victim is that the martyr

> chooses to be sacrificed, or rather – and in this he resembles the Epic Hero – it is his destiny to be sacrificed and he accepts his destiny. Those for whose sake he sacrifices himself do not choose him as an atoning sacrifice; on the contrary, they deny that any sacrifice has been made. To them, he is a criminal, blasphemer, disturber of the social order . . . (16–17)

The martyr is a wholly conscious, self-righteous person who carries the moral burden for the situation which his or her actions have precipitated. The martyr's suffering, unlike the victim's, is not a sign of a lack of control; it constitutes proof of a mastery of events and of an invincibility of spirit. Martyr protagonists affirm their freedom through actions into which they enter by choice and which result in their suffering. The suffering of victims alerts us to the existence of evil but does not tell us anything about the character of the protagonist; by contrast, the suffering of martyrs is fraught with meaning because martyrs choose to suffer and to sacrifice themselves to an ideal which the audience is meant to share, or at least admire.

The question whether the saint, the martyr figure or even the person of seemingly total innocence can be considered tragic has been much debated since Aristotle's *Poetics*, partly because of the dramatically problematic nature of goodness. The totally blameless character is usually excluded from the category of the ideal hero. We may recall Butcher's discussion of Aristotle in this connection. In *Aristotle's Theory of Poetry and Fine Art* (1895), Butcher maintains that according to Aristotle, the totally blameless character is 'unfit to be a tragic hero on the ground that wholly unmerited suffering causes repulsion; not fear or pity' (308). In other words, the dramatization of innocence victimized does not elicit a tragic response. Butcher further argues for excluding the guiltless character from tragedy on the technical grounds that total goodness lacks the dramatic energy which propels the hero and results in action and in a collision. The man or woman of complete innocence lacks 'self-assertive energy' (310). Essentially inert, goodness 'with its unselfish, self-effacing tendency, is apt to be immobile and uncombative. In refusing to strike back it brings the action to a standstill' (310). Hence Butcher believes that goodness and guiltlessness are inherently non-dramatic.

He cites Antigone as a good example of the innocent tragic character, but concedes that, on the whole, Aristotle's 'reluctance to admit a perfect character to the place of the protagonist has been almost justified by the history of tragic drama' (310). Of course, the question of guilt is itself complex and dependent upon the audience's perspective. To say that Antigone is innocent is to ignore the historical and political context the playwright establishes and within which the character's actions must be judged. In the eyes of her society, Antigone is both innocent and guilty; indeed, this duality constitutes the tragic tension and leads to her demise.

When considering the question of guilt in *The Crucible*, for instance, one must realize that in the historical context of seventeenth-century Salem the hysteria concerning witchcraft is no less 'real' than that concerning Communists during the McCarthy era. Eric Bentley's objection, in 'The Innocence of Arthur Miller', that Proctor's innocence is total and unreal because his crime is fabricated bespeaks an anachronistic reading of the play (62–5). Proctor's crime is no more fabricated than Antigone's. Although Miller draws the analogy between the Salem witchhunts and the McCarthy era in order to demonstrate to modern audiences the baselessness of the 1950s accusations and their witchhunt atmosphere, in order for the comparison to be effective, one must first suspend disbelief and accept the plausibility of witchcraft, at least for the duration of the play. Furthermore, one must also accept the reality of Proctor's sinfulness in order to understand his actions. The success of the play depends first and foremost on one's acceptance of certain unacceptable ideas and on one's ability to respond to Miller's brand of 'making strange', that is, viewing something recent and familiar in terms of something distant and unfamiliar. Miller draws the analogy between the historical situation and the contemporary one in order to force the audience to take a fresh look at a political phenomenon and to see one persecution in terms of another.

Like blameless figures, martyrs are equally unsuited to being tragic heroes, Butcher asserts. Although they do not lack strong initiative, they are forces, personifications of ideals rather than individuals. In a very restrictive definition of martyrdom and one which does not allow for formal variations, he maintains that the martyr's

> impersonal ardour in the cause of right has not the same dramatic fascination as the spectacle of human weakness or passion doing battle with the fate it has brought upon itself. (311)

However, one may argue that the fanaticism entailed in 'impersonal ardour in the cause of right' need be no less dramatically intense or fear-engendering than 'human weakness or passion' precipitating a fateful event. Regardless of the impersonality of the initial impulse to action, the retribution cannot but be personal. (In Shaw's *Saint Joan*, Cauchon's assertion to the ghost of Joan that the burning was not personal, but merely political, surely cannot be taken at face value.) Butcher further asserts that the martyr play is much too unequivocally affirmative to be tragic: the martyr's death 'fills us with emotions of wonder and admiration; but can hardly produce the thrill of fear or tragic awe' (311–12). In other words, the martyr play cannot elicit tragic emotions in the spectator because the martyr is too removed from ordinary humanity to have dramatic interest.

Finally, according to Butcher, tragedy must, while recognizing and even celebrating individualism, have a humbling effect on the individual ego because, he says,

> tragedy, in its pure idea, shows us a mortal will engaged in an unequal struggle with destiny, whether that destiny be represented by the forces within or without the mind. The conflict reaches its tragic issue when the individual perishes, but through his ruin the disturbed order of the world is restored and the moral forces reassert their sway.

Individualism, even as kind and selfless as Cordelia's, is ultimately punished in a tragedy. By contrast, the martyr play is the quintessential drama of individualism:

> The death of the martyr presents to us not the defeat, but the victory of the individual; the issue of a conflict in which the

> individual is ranged on the same side as the higher powers, and the sense of suffering consequently lost in that of moral triumph. (311–12)

Butcher notes that the martyr play's glorification of the individual and of individualism at the expense of the greater order, as well as its identification of the martyr with the higher moral powers, renders it incompatible with tragedy's requirements. However, it is precisely these qualities of the drama of martyrdom – in a somewhat modified form – that make it compatible with some modern versions of tragedy where the self-righteous hero, existing in an essentially meaningless universe, is ranged on the side of ethical virtue and stands opposed to a corrupt social and moral (dis)order.

Anderson's *Journey to Jerusalem* (1940) and *Joan of Lorraine* (1946), Miller's *The Crucible* (1953) and Williams' *Orpheus Descending* (1957), as well as *Death of a Salesman* and *A Streetcar Named Desire*, to mention just a few, are variations on the theme of the faith-filled hero confronting a faithless society. The idealist hero is like a lone martyr in a lost, but ultimately triumphant, battle with a spiritually bankrupt community. The dramatization of his or her destruction provides the spectator with the affirmation required of tragedy. By virtue of his or her opposition to a fallen world, an extreme sensitivity to evil and an affinity with higher moral powers, the martyr partakes of a heroic quality that Louis L. Martz, in his essay 'The Saint as Tragic Hero', refers to as 'saintliness', the concept of saintliness having of course undergone considerable redefinition. In an attempt to demonstrate the close relationship between the saint play and tragedy, Martz extends the definition of saintliness to include tragic heroes such as Hamlet and Oedipus (in *Oedipus at Colonus*) and uses the term to refer to moral qualities. But it is not to be confused with moral perfection nor with total blamelessness, nor is distancing from evil to be equated with total innocence. Thus saintliness is applicable to a large spectrum of personalities who do not necessarily exemplify actual martyrdom but who, due to their moral sensibility, earn the epithet 'saintly'.

Martz's discussion of the close relationship between the saint play and tragedy serves as a useful antidote to Butcher's rigid categorization. While re-examining the saint play, he also expands the definition of tragedy in order to accommodate a wide range of modern drama where the hero partakes of the special traits of the martyr. Specifically, he analyses the modern saint play (using as examples Shaw's *Saint Joan* and Eliot's *Murder in the Cathedral*) which is dominated by a much greater degree of skepticism than the conventional saint play and is plagued by some of the same technical problems as modern tragedy. Both Shaw's and Eliot's plays may be seen as plays of faith in a faithless age and, as a result, as embodying an essentially tragic tension, something not necessarily associated with the saint play. Martz chooses to focus on the tragic element in the modern martyr play, on the struggle between faith and doubt, and to examine the point at which tragedy and martyrdom intersect in the modern imagination.

His underlying assumption – one that is shared by many modern critics writing about the nature of tragedy – is that tragedy is to be found in a double vision which encompasses disillusionment as well as affirmation, and which shows both 'the human sufferer' and 'the secret cause'. He borrows these last two categories from Stephen Dedalus' definition of tragedy in Joyce's *A Portrait of the Artist as a Young Man* and has the following passage in mind:

> Pity is the feeling which arrests the mind in the presence of whatsoever is grave and constant in human sufferings and unites it with the human sufferer. Terror is the feeling which arrests the mind in the presence of whatsoever is grave and constant in human sufferings and unites it with the secret cause. (204)

Martz then states that tragedy

> seems to demand both the human sufferer and the secret cause: that is to say, the doubt, the pain, the pity of the human sufferer; and the affirmation, the awe, the terror of the secret cause. It is an affirmation even though the cause is destructive in its immediate effects: for this cause seems to affirm the existence of some universal order of things. (153)

Like tragedy, the martyr play embodies the categories of 'the secret cause' and 'the human sufferer' which are directly related to the Aristotelian tragic sentiments of terror and pity respectively.

Martz also ascribes this double vision to the saint play. In tragedy, the double vision or tension is contained within the figure of the divided hero; in the saint play, however, the martyr is the sole receptacle of the secret cause, and the people (the chorus) represent the human sufferers, or pity and doubt. Martz argues that one must look 'for a tragic experience that arises from the interaction between a hero who represents the secret cause, and the other characters, who represent the human sufferers' (158). In such situations, the conflict between the martyr's faithful dedication to a cause and the people's skepticism constitutes the tragic tension. Referring to Shaw's *Saint Joan,* Martz comments that 'some degree of tragedy resides in . . . [the] failure of Everyman to recognize Absolute Reality, the secret cause, when it appears in the flesh' (160).

Modern plays of martyrdom show the tragedy not only of the heroic individual, but also of the persecuting society. They echo Cauchon's outcry in the Epilogue of Shaw's play: 'Must then a Christ perish in torment in every age to save those that have no imagination?' Although modern plays of martyrdom carry an indictment of the society that would destroy all who oppose it, they also reaffirm the potential for value and passion in a world considered devoid of meaning. The tension characterizing the drama of faith in a faithless age is not only between doubt and faith but also between individual expression and social responsibility. The martyr is motivated by a whole spectrum of impulses ranging from the most asocially individualistic and egoistic to the social and profoundly selfless. Hence martyrdom, as a dramatic construct, has a strong appeal for the modern playwright interested in tragedy. The martyr play is both consciously social and supremely individualistic; therefore, it successfully bridges the rift between private concerns and public realities, and even more interestingly, allows for the disguise of the public as private, and vice versa.

Through the agency of the secret cause (which he uses in the wide sense of a moral realm, as well as of an absolute reality in touch with the mysteries of existence) Martz implies a close relationship not only between tragedy and the martyr play, but also between the modern serious play and the saint play and, indirectly, between the modern serious play and tragedy. Central to all these dramatic forms is the sense of mystery and the exploration of a moral realm.[1]

Another very important element in the historical martyr play, not mentioned by Butcher, is the role played by posterity. The intransigent society which the hero-martyr opposes is shown by posterity to be in the wrong and the martyr is vindicated. The martyr play is a restatement of that vindication by posterity. Indeed, this vindication is sometimes complete and, as a result, posterity may fail to understand the issue of guilt and may declare the character's total innocence. Although the drama of martyrdom replays the victimization of an outcast individual, it in fact celebrates a rehabilitated person and in this manner merges victim and victor in the character of the hero. Thus the character is a vanquished victim when viewed in terms of his or her former transgression and defeat, but a victor when seen by posterity as having vanquished the forces of evil through self-destructive action. Indeed, the martyr's dramatic identity is dependent on this dialogue between past and present, defeat and victory, guilt and innocence. It is these dualities that plays such as *The Crucible, Journey to Jerusalem* and *Joan of Lorraine* explore.

In *The Crucible,* for instance, the entire environment is condemned by the playwright, and the protagonist's actions are reinterpreted by a modern audience that brings to the theatre its particular historical and political understanding. By contrast, the actions of traditional tragic heroes do not call for vindication by posterity because they do not undergo transformation through dramatization. For instance, although Lear's actions and reactions are context-bound – that is, intelligible in the context of his and Shakespeare's socio-political environment and contingent on a particular understanding of both social relations and drama – his tragic error remains equally erroneous through time and with each reenactment; the larger social and moral framework is not on trial in the drama.

The Epilogue in Shaw's *Saint Joan* is particularly effective in its delineation of the interplay between initial perceptions of guilt and those following the blasphemer's vindication. The play exposes not only the historical persecution of an undoubtedly subversive element, but also the later rehabilitation and canonization of a wronged person. By depicting the entire spectrum of historical developments, Shaw illustrates the contextual and shifting nature of innocence and guilt as he dramatizes the creation of saints in a changing society and, by implication, the making and unmaking of heroes.

Martz's discussion of the tension between doubt and faith in the saint play is of particular relevance to Anderson's understanding of the tragic hero. The protagonist's spiritual awakening is the essence of tragedy; the audience's raising of moral consciousness and affirmation of its faith is tragedy's goal, according to Anderson. In terms of construction,

> A play should lead up to and away from a central crisis, and this crisis should consist in a discovery by the leading character which

> has an indelible effect on his thought and emotion and completely alters his course of action. The leading character . . . must make the discovery; it must affect him emotionally; and it must alter his direction in the play. ('The Essence of Tragedy', 7)

The discovery invariably involves a moral imperative. For example, when Essex (in *Elizabeth the Queen*) discovers that he loves the Queen and that he also loves power, he undergoes a crisis and this leads to an alteration in his course of action, which in turn results in his giving up his life to preserve his honor. In the case of *Elizabeth the Queen*, the protagonist is made aware of his desires and of political realities. In other plays, the gained understanding may be of a more spiritual nature, such as young Jesus' growing awareness and acceptance of his messianic role in *Journey to Jerusalem*. That Anderson emphasizes the central discovery over, for example, intensity of action, suffering or destruction, as the essential element of tragedy, is indicative of the didactic function he attributes to theatre. He insists that the protagonist have admirable qualities, that he be on the side of good, that he have moral excellence – but not be perfect, for there must be room for improvement – and finally, that a healthy moral atmosphere prevail. In the course of the play, the hero's character must be 'tried in the fire' ('Off Broadway', 24–6) Anderson insists.

It is not surprising, therefore, that Anderson should choose historical martyrs for his exemplary and virtuous heroes. Jeshua (*Journey to Jerusalem*) and Joan (*Joan of Lorraine*) are the type of great spirit Anderson has in mind when he writes in 'Whatever Hope We Have' that

> the world we live in is given meaning and dignity, is made an endurable habitation, by the great spirits who have preceded us and set down their records of nobility or torture or defeat in blazons and symbols which we can understand. (21)

Through the dramatization of the actions and fate of these great spirits Anderson hopes to inculcate a need for heroism.

Faced with the spectre of Nazism, Anderson turns in *Journey to Jerusalem* (1940) to the story of young Jesus for hope and inspiration. Religion *per se* is not what Anderson champions in the play; rather, Christianity is used to provide a historical instance of bourgeoning faith 'at a time when despair and unfaith had gripped Jesus's own people, when the Roman Empire, ruled by sensualists and materialists, hung over a world of doubting and cynical slave-states' (Preface, *Journey to Jerusalem*). Anderson sees similarities between that period in history and his own times; thus his 'version of the mystery of the emergence of Jesus' (Preface, 213) serves as a call to spiritual awakening at a critical time.

In a curious, but by no means unusual, leap of logic, he equates political brutality with reliance on scientific values and, by association, with spiritual bankruptcy. Therefore, for Anderson, the most dangerous form of materialism and faithlessness is exemplified by Nazism. (He overlooks the fact that fanatic faith was not only the basis of Nazism but its most sinister weapon.) He considers the contemporary situation to be an outgrowth of utter despair and cynicism. Whereas in *Key Largo* his solution to fascism is struggle, in *Journey to Jerusalem* it seems to be faith.

The rule of force, Anderson claims, can exist only 'in a despairing nation, a nation of men who have lost faith in their dignity and destiny' (Preface, 211). Therefore the only answer to political terror and brutality is 'some kind of faith, faith of men in themselves and in the race of men' (212). To emerge out of this period of skepticism and despair, humanity must once again 'believe that there is purpose and pattern in the universe . . . that every individual man has a sacred right to follow his own intuition toward that purpose' (212). People must discover values beyond scientific ones, for 'the only sources of human dignity and respect for the individual are the great arts, such as poetry, and the great religions, such as Christianity' (212). He maintains that those who 'believe in salvation by science and machinery' (212) do not constitute a viable opposition to the rule of force, whether in the form of Herod or Hitler. He sees religion as one possible type of faith and martyrdom as an exemplum of self-sacrifice for a cause.

Journey to Jerusalem dramatizes the thirteen-year-old Jesus' growing awareness of immense responsibility which, Anderson explains in the Preface, symbolizes 'the soul of man searching for its own meaning' (214). The play centres on that period in Jeshua's young life when he discovers that he is the Messiah. The prophet Ishmael explains to the young Jeshua his future conquest and describes the Messiah as judge, deliverer and martyr:

> The Messiah is sent to hunt out wisdom and truth,
> to speak this wisdom and truth in love to those
> who need his love, and in bitterness to those

> who have earned bitterness. And in the end
> for this love and bitterness with which he speaks
> he will become a symbol of those who are guiltless –
> and those who are guilty, seeing in him this symbol,
> will turn and destroy him. He will suffer for them
> and conquer them in their hearts.
> (273)

At this point Jeshua protests against accepting the mission:

> No, I cannot! I cannot!
> I have never borne pain! I cannot bear pain!
> And I'm afraid of death!
> I cannot face death! I say this is not for me –
> to be this Messiah!
> (274)

But Ishmael insists that 'there's no turning back once I've spoken to you' (271). It is his mission, he says

> to fill your soul
> with a torment that will become an exaltation –
> because it is your mission to torment
> the earth, and exalt it.
> (271)

Jeshua gradually comes to understand his responsibility of fulfilling a role which is heroic and tragic in its inevitable doom and victory.

Although the play is of course neither a tragedy nor a martyr play – it only prophesies martyrdom – the sacrificial protagonist's faithful acceptance of a predicament whose very essence is victory in defeat is essentially tragic. The hero's prophesied regeneration and bringing of justice reaffirms, through its global significance, Anderson's faith. At the same time, it emphasizes the great capacity for suffering, itself a mark of the tragic hero. The person of faith, here and in Anderson's other plays, functions as an emblem of hope. For example, in *Key Largo* King McCloud progresses from disbelief through commitment to self-sacrifice, albeit on a smaller, more personal scale than Jeshua, and through his character Anderson dramatizes the need for hope in the midst of hopelessness. For

McCloud, the sacrifice signifies both an affirmation of personal faith and a struggle for a cause. In *Key Largo* the emphasis is on the growing sense of responsibility and on the acceptance of the heroic role of martyrdom.

In the rehearsal play *Joan of Lorraine* (1946) Anderson alternates between showing a present day theatre company's preparations for a play about Joan of Arc and dramatizing the martyr play. The martyr's grand-scale struggle and trial are echoed in the petty daily trials of the actors, as Anderson draws a parallel between Saint Joan's heroic martyrdom and the ethical and aesthetic concerns of the actress playing Joan.

The play-within-a-play functions as a learning device and serves as a behavioural model for its actors. Anderson believes that due to the pettiness of modern concerns and the ordinariness of contemporary characters, heroism is not conceivable on the modern stage. What is possible, however, is for Mary, the actress playing Joan, to reach a moment of illumination and spiritual awakening through her dramatic recreation of historical martyrdom. By superimposing a figure from former, more heroic, times onto an ambitious present day character, Anderson makes a statement about faith and dedication to a cause that is relevant for his own historical situation.

Mary must come to terms with the disturbing concessions the theatre company must make as well as with the play's pessimistic message. At one point she is ready to capitulate. After a short absence, she returns fully cognizant of her 'calling' and accepts some loss of naïve illusion in order to faithfully create a work of art. On a very different scale, Joan gradually comprehends her responsibility and realizes in the process that victory is not beautiful, but 'ugly and bloody and hateful' (44). Nonetheless, or perhaps precisely for this reason, she is determined to follow her faith to the fire. The loss of illusion makes her more determined. Unlike prince Rudolph, she does not capitulate but is willing to become tainted with victory, like King McCloud. In *Joan of Lorraine,* as well as in *Journey to Jerusalem* and in *Key Largo,* the transition from innocent faith and hope through loss of illusion to experienced faith must precede martyrdom. The defeatist hero moves from loss of illusion to disillusion; the true martyr progresses from loss of illusion to faithful dedication.

Anderson limits Joan's dramatic development by focusing throughout the play primarily on Mary and on her reaction to the character she portrays. Trying to understand this character, Mary states that Joan illustrates

> that the great things in this world are brought about by faith – that all the leaders who count are dreamers and people who see visions. The realists and common-sense people can never begin anything. They can only do what the visionaries plan for them. The scientists can never lead unless they happen to be dreamers, too. (50)

Thus Joan, the hope for a despairing world, is portrayed as a visionary and a dreamer, rather than the tough political realist and strategist she may have been. Once again, Anderson reiterates the need for faith, visions and dreams in a materialistic world. Masters, the theatre director in the play and the mouthpiece for Anderson's ideas, says, echoing d'Alcala of *Key Largo*:

> . . . it's our destiny to be in the dark and yet go forward – to doubt our religions and yet live by them. To know that our faith can't be proved and yet to stick to it. (58)

The Andersonian credo, 'faith in things unseen', is the play's slogan for a war-torn world.

The play is open-ended: it closes with Joan or, more precisely, with Mary in the role of Joan. Thus Anderson succeeds in showing heroism on the contemporary stage. Although Mary's determination may seem trite juxtaposed with Joan's genuine heroism, by portraying Joan, Mary participates in heroism and is given a chance to understand it. The final affirmation comes from the historical martyr: 'And if it were to do over, I would do it again. I would follow my faith, even to the fire' (90). Through this device, the heroic lines are uttered by the modern character who thus 'becomes' the martyr without straining the credulity of a modern audience.

The idea of martyrdom lends itself also to a liberal-humanist interpretations of heroism and suffering. As Raymond Williams contends in *Modern Tragedy*, during the nineteenth century the identification of the hypocritical, false society as the enemy of the individual facilitated the transformation of the bourgeois hero-as-victim into the hero-as-rebel against the hostile society. It was also at this time that the figure of the 'liberal martyr' or 'the heroic liberator opposed and destroyed by a false society' (97) emerged. He identifies John Proctor in *The Crucible* as a 'liberal martyr', both a victim of society and a potential deliverer – through sacrificial death – of its people. Raymond Williams' description of the 'liberal martyr' is also appropriate for the saviour/sacrificial figure who combines the traits of both victim and victor and is destroyed as he or she stages a profoundly anti-social and personal rebellion which has its social ramifications.

The Crucible (1953) embodies the duality of private and social motivation and the inherent tension. Although John Proctor's action serves a social cause – he sacrifices himself in order to save others and to stage a protest against his persecutors – he is driven essentially by the impulse to preserve his integrity as well as by the need to expiate his sin. By showing how mass hysteria feeds on private guilt and encourages private vengeance under the guise of self-righteous public accusation, the play examines that point where social imperatives impinge upon individual freedom.

A jilted lover accuses Proctor of witchcraft, a very real accusation in the context of seventeenth-century Salem, regardless of twentieth-century attitudes. A paranoid society has condemned Proctor, but he has also condemned himself. He may not actually be guilty of witchcraft, but he does carry the burden of guilt for his adultery. In a number of Miller's plays, especially where adultery plays a central role, for example in *Death of a Salesman, After the Fall* and *The Crucible,* personal guilt is often externalized as public guilt, and social morality is reflected in, and often equated with, individual morality. In a lengthy, virtually Shavian stage direction, Miller describes Proctor as

> *a sinner, a sinner not only against the moral fashion of the time, but against his own vision of decent conduct . . . . Proctor, respected and even feared in Salem, has come to regard himself as a kind of fraud.* (239)

Proctor's trial by the community is subordinate to his tense trial of conscience in a drama in which self-examination, judgement and acceptance of responsibility during personal and societal crisis play an important role.

Proctor is faced with a dilemma: he can save his life if he confesses and betrays others, or he can sacrifice his life to his ideals. He struggles with his conscience and, knowing that he is morally blemished by adultery, thinks he cannot justify a proud sacrifice or a false heroism. He feels unworthy of his propensity for martyrdom: 'I cannot mount the gibbet like a saint. It is a fraud. I am not that man' (322), he objects. After considerable self-examination, he is willing to renounce his beliefs, to confess to his sins. However, when he realizes that he is expected to give up his confession to public use, he protests: 'You will not use me! . . . It is no part of salvation that you should use me' (327). After having put his signature to the recantation, he asks for his name back:

> Because it is my name! Because I cannot have another in my life! Because I lie and sign myself to lies! Because I am not worth the dust on the feet of them that hang! How may I live without my name? I have given you my soul; leave me my name! (328)

Proctor comes face to face with the machinations of the community as he realizes that in order to save his life, he must side with the forces of evil. It is then that he decides to doff his guilty conscience and stand up to his persecutors.

Throughout his critical writings, and especially in 'The Shadows of the Gods', Miller criticizes the narrow – usually psychological – focus of contemporary theatre. He calls for greater emphasis on ultimate causes rather than mere effects. The modern preoccupation with the psyche of the alienated, frustrated individual must necessarily result, he says, in an impoverished dramatic vision and a loss of poetic power. As a consequence, in the 'Introduction to the Collected Plays', he insists that for modern drama to be faithful to reality, it must embrace 'both determinism and the paradox of will', because the unfortunate split between the private and the public domains results in a typically modern paradoxical need to 'write of private persons privately and lift up their means of expression to a poetic – that is, a social – level' ('On Social Plays', 57). The realistic mode – a consciously created style best suited to the presentation of family relations and to individual psychological characterization – is inherently prosaic; only the dramatization of social relations, of a conflict of forces, of larger truths of existence – expressed in anti-realistic, expressionist modes – has poetic potential ('The Family in Modern Drama'). Miller believes that the contemporary playwright who explores only the private mask and loses sight of the public individual inevitably remains earth-bound, for

> the current quest after the poetic as poetic is fruitless. It is an attempt to make apples grow without growing trees. It is seeking poetry precisely where poetry is not: in the private life viewed entirely within the bounds of the subjective, the area of

sensation, or the bizarre and the erotic. ('The Family in Modern Drama', 82)

The truly poetic – here he differentiates between the genuinely poetic and the merely lyrical – must be born of a balance between the private and the public and be a dramatic presentation of the whole person.

In *The Crucible* Miller emphasizes Proctor's increasing awareness of the interaction between private and public masks and dramatizes the initially-reluctant acceptance of the heroic role and of the martyr's fate following the painful process of self-scrutiny. Central to the play is Miller's idea that at certain times in history, at 'sharp' times as Deputy Governor Danforth calls them, humanity perceives two irreconcilable opposites operating in the world. It is at such crucial moments in the life of the community, 'when an individual conscience . . . [is] all that . . . [can] keep a world from falling' (*Timebends*, 342), that the individual must make a clear choice. Through his refusal to name names and betray others, Proctor defines himself as a good man, perhaps the only sane man in an insane universe which has condemned him. He emerges from the crucible of his conscience a changed man; his character, like that of the Andersonian tragic hero, is 'tried in the fire'.

It is questionable whether Proctor's proud acceptance of death partakes of the heroism Butcher calls 'impersonal ardour in the cause of right'. Although he selflessly refuses to turn against his friends and neighbours, it is in fact his personal integrity that is at stake if he recants and confesses. Proctor's motivation is individualistic rather than genuinely social and akin to what Raymond Williams, in his *Modern Tragedy*, calls 'personal verification by death' (104). Such diverse characters as Rudolph (in *The Masque of Kings*), Essex and Willy all verify their identity through death and share a suicidal tendency which Williams considers to be 'the last stage of liberal tragedy' (*Modern Tragedy*, 104).

Miller, too, has pointed out that his ultimate concern was with the assault on the identity of the individual in a socially hostile situation. He

wished for a way to write a play that would be sharp, that would lift out of the morass of subjectivism that squirming, single, defined process which would show that the sin of public terror

> is that it divests man of conscience of himself. ('Introduction to the Collected Plays', 40–1)

In Proctor's circumstances, the only means of regaining this integrity is through death. Essentially all martyrs find themselves in a similar predicament. This play, like a number of others, explores the possibility of maintaining individual integrity in an oppressive environment. Therefore, the outsider's private rebellion has public significance precisely because it is individualistic. That is, by insisting on their individuality, martyr figures stage a protest against public norms and expectations.

In a further development of liberal tragedy, the figure of the martyr is often related to that of the scapegoat; indeed, the hero may be presented as a persecuted outsider, a sacrificial victim of society and at the same time someone of heightened sensibility and superior conscience who chooses his or her fate. Frye suggests in *Anatomy of Criticism* that

> the figure of a typical or random victim begins to crystallize in domestic tragedy as it deepens in ironic tone. We may call this typical victim the *pharmakos* or scapegoat. We meet a *pharmakos* figure in Hawthorne's Hester Prynne, in Melville's Billy Budd, in Hardy's Tess, in the Septimus of *Mrs. Dalloway*, in the stories of persecuted Jews and Negroes, in the stories of artists whose genius makes them Ishmaels of a bourgeois society. The *pharmakos* is neither innocent nor guilty. He is innocent in the sense that what happens to him is far greater than anything he has done provokes, like the mountaineer whose shout brings down an avalanche. He is guilty in the sense that he is a member of a guilty society, or living in a world where such injustices are an inescapable part of existence. (41)

The ambivalence of guilt and the complexity of innocence figure frequently in the plays of O'Neill, Miller and Williams where the characters' punishments far exceed their crimes and where their existential unease is a function of their complicity in a valueless world.

In some of his plays Williams gives the scapegoat the characteristics of the martyr and confers dignity upon his 'fugitive kind' – the persecuted artist or the person of heightened sensitivity and moral awareness victimized and destroyed by a materialistic, philistine society – by emphasizing their suffering and their uncompromising position. In *Orpheus Descending* (1957), in the figure of Valentine Xavier, itinerant guitarist who descends into the underworld of a small southern town, Williams merges martyr, scapegoat and deliverer. Val's journey into the town, his attempted rescue of Lady Torrence – a woman at odds with her community – and his pursuit by a lynch mob at the end parallel Orpheus' descent into the underworld, his attempt to rescue Eurydice, and his dismemberment by the Thracians.

In a 1957 interview, Williams stated that the play deals with 'what . . . is corrupt in life' (Devlin, 42) and a year later, in his Preface to *Orpheus Descending*, described it in the following manner:

> On the surface it . . . is the tale of a wild-spirited boy who wanders into a conventional community of the South and creates the commotion of a fox in a chicken coop.
>
> But beneath that . . . surface it is a play about unanswered questions that haunt the hearts of people and the difference between continuing to ask them, a difference represented by the four major protagonists of the play, and the acceptance of prescribed answers that are not answers at all, but expedient adaptations or surrender to a state of quandary. (vi)

Such an account is just a partial description of a play characterized not so much by questions and answers, but by violent action and an undercurrent of frustration and despair. The Southern town in which Val/Orpheus finds himself is a corrupt, suffocating underworld eager to destroy the outsider. Williams indicates in the stage directions that the setting and atmosphere of *Orpheus Descending* are increasingly less and less realistic and more witchlike (122). He transforms a morally decayed community, what C. W. E. Bigsby has called a 'disintegrating structure' (1984, 2:98) into the setting for the ritualistic sacrifice of an intruder who would bring life and love to a community permeated by pain and death.

Val Xavier, with *'a kind of wild beauty about him'* (16) becomes the last hope for the Eurydice character Lady Torrence. Her father 'the wop bootlegger', was burned alive by the 'mystic crew', a Ku Klux Klan type organization led by her husband, Jabe Torrence. This is just one of the horrors in the recent history of a town torn by intolerance, hatred and violence. Throughout the play can be heard the baying of dogs in pursuit of fugitives, ready to tear them to pieces.

Williams describes Jabe, the owner of the general store which constitutes the setting of the play, as *'death's self, and malignancy'* (114). His dying, like Big Daddy's in *Cat on a Hot Tin Roof*, symbolizes corruption and decay, in this case of a town which is in the grips of the kind of violence Val describes as quick, as well as the other kind, which 'ain't quick always'. Like corruption, 'it's slow. Some tornadoes are slow. Corruption – rots men's hearts and – rot is slow' (67). Purified by his art, his guitar, Val has remained untouched by evil. As he admits,

> I lived in corruption but I'm not corrupted. Here is why. [*Picks up his guitar.*] My life's companion! It washes me clean like water when anything unclean has touched me. (37)

Because he is a visionary and a potentially life-giving force, he is pursued by three women of the town, all three outsiders. It is their interest in him that turns the men of the community against Val. He tells Lady Torrence that 'there's just two kinds of people, the ones that are bought and the buyers! No! – there's one other kind . . . the kind that's never been branded' (41). Val aspires to being this third kind. His vision of freedom is a tiny, delicate bird without feet who hovers above the ground and is destroyed when he touches it. In the end, Val is branded and destroyed by a mob of men carrying blow-torches.

Considering Blanche DuBois a similar victim of her environment, Williams said in an interview that 'She was not adaptable to the circumstances as they were, that the world had imposed on her. She was a sacrificial victim . . . ; she was metaphorical as a sacrificial victim of society' (Devlin, 277). In her confrontation with Stanley, Blanche becomes a scapegoat of the brutish society he embodies and Stella passively accepts. Her rape by Stanley, which precipitates her mental disintegration, sums up this relationship between the group and the scapegoat. She must be sacrificed in order not to threaten Stanley and Stella's relationship; in another sense, she must be sacrificed because she is the outsider whose destruction confirms the cohesiveness of the group. Because she chooses to put herself into this position, to seek out her 'executioner' and to undergo the suffering that awaits her from the beginning of her quest, she resembles the martyr figures who, in turn, preserve their integrity by remaining outsiders and allowing themselves to be destroyed by the mob. Williams raises the sacrificial victim to the level of the martyr and thus de-objectifies her. In other words, he endows her with the self-consciousness and determination that an ordinary victim usually lacks.

Frye believes that in the ironic stage of tragedy, the enemy of the individual is the mob, 'which is essentially human society looking for a *pharmakos*' (149) – and, one may add, in the case of some plays, the *pharmakos* looking for the destructive human society. The mob's destruction of the scapegoat entails

> the imagery of cannibalism [which] usually includes, not only images of torture and mutilation, but of what is technically known as *sparagmos* or the tearing apart of the sacrificial body, an image found in the myths of Osiris, Orpheus, and Penteus. (148)

For Stanley Kowalski, representative of the mob, Blanche is just such a sacrificial body to be desecrated and discarded. Although not physically torn apart in the manner of Orpheus for instance, Blanche is physically violated and psychically 'dismembered'.

Although characters such as Val Xavier, Chris Keller, Willy Loman, Blanche DuBois or King McCloud are concerned primarily with self-definition in a world depriving them of identity and of dignity, they stand for a set of values espoused by the dramatist in opposition to the social norm. They may not articulate their suffering clearly, but they undergo anguish for a cause in a setting where causes no longer seem to matter. Charlie, in *Death of a Salesman*, appropriately exemplifies the cynicism inherent in the pursuit of material wealth. This well-adjusted man tells the desperate Willy: 'My salvation is that I never took any interest in anything' (191). Willy, on the other hand, is not 'saved' in this manner: he is unwilling and unable to relinquish his dreams about the past or his visions of the future. In a world exemplified by Charlie, any intense interest and any faith – whether religious, ethical, aesthetic, social or political – must have its price. In a materialistic world, the personal protests of Blanche, Willy and Val Xavier acquire wider and impersonal implications and may conceivably be seen as modern equivalents to martyrdom. Although the protest against dehumanization is presented in very personal terms in *Death of a Salesman,* Willy is sacrificed not only to his own misrepresentation of societal values and to an intense but misplaced idealism, but also to a larger protest against the social system. Similarly, Blanche's sacrifice to her mad intensity may be seen as American culture's martyrdom at the hands of the philistines. Harold Bloom calls Blanche 'a failed Whitmanian' and comments that:

> The fall of Blanche is a parable, not of American civilization's lost nobility, but of the failure of the American literary imagination to rise above its recent myths of recurrent defeat. (Tennessee Williams' *A Streetcar Named Desire*, 40)

In this interpretation, Blanche is a failed artistic figure, a would-be romantic; and 'though Blanche yearns for the values of the aesthetic, she scarcely embodies them, being in this failure a masochistic self-parody on the part of Williams himself' (4). Bloom's analysis takes one not only from the private (Blanche) to the social and emblematic (America) but back to the private, to a self-portrait of the presumably anguished playwright.

Perhaps the best way to summarize the nature of the idealist's battle is to point out that whereas the tragic hero disrupts the existing order – which in a tragedy may be questioned or tested but which is always reaffirmed in the end – the modern hero/martyr stages a self-destructive protest against the order by refusing to be an integral part of it. Furthermore, the ethical values of the vanquishing order are rejected as the protagonist's moral superiority is affirmed in his or her destruction.

It is fitting that in an anti-heroic and skeptical age dramatists should turn to the depiction of martyrdom (whether actual or perceived), a form of heroism characterized by extreme individualism on one end of the spectrum and by social commitment on the other and, furthermore, a heroism which may be subversive due to its anti-authoritarian nature. Bernard Shaw's distinction between official greatness (or power) and unofficial greatness (or intellectual and spiritual superiority) may be useful here to illustrate the type of heroism one encounters in these modern plays. It is unofficial greatness, Shaw explains, that is deemed subversive and is therefore suppressed by the authorities:

> The legal and conventional superiority of Herod and Pilate, and of Annas and Caiaphas, inspires fear; but the fear, being reasonable fear of measurable and avoidable consequences which seem salutary and protective, is bearable; whilst the strange superiority of Christ and the fear it inspires elicit a shriek of Crucify Him from all who cannot divine its benevolence. (*Saint Joan*, 267–8)

This spiritual and intellectual – as opposed to political – power, which Shaw calls 'strange superiority', is the domain of those to whom Martz refers as saintly; and perhaps, on a smaller scale, those whom Miller and Williams consider heroic also partake of such unofficial and potentially subversive greatness. Of course, Blanche DuBois, Willy Loman and Val Xavier do not belong in the same category as historic martyrs; nonetheless, within the small worlds depicted by Miller and Williams, they are the representatives of the unofficial opposition to power. They engage in ordinary struggles in an everyday environment where Stanley Kowalski, Willy's boss Howard and Jabe Torrence constitute power and represent the official view. Thus minor heroes such as Blanche, Willy or even Val Xavier hardly qualify as embodiments of the 'secret cause'; nonetheless, their separateness from Everyman or Everywoman marks them as gauges of society's intolerance.

Butcher suggests three characteristics of martyr drama: first, the individual is victorious; second, the individual is at one with a higher moral order; finally, as a result, the play ends in moral triumph for the individual. Whereas in tragedy the society or the world at large represents the moral order and is ranged on the same side as the higher powers, in the martyr play the martyr is the representative of the moral order and stands in opposition to a hostile society. Although the individual suffers and often perishes in the struggle, it is the society which, in final analysis, is vanquished and whose values are questioned. By dramatizing the suffering of historical martyrs, in plays such as *The Crucible, Journey to Jerusalem* and *Joan of Lorraine,* Miller and Anderson bring to the modern stage a heroic intensity having social ramifications supposedly inconceivable in a contemporary setting. By contrast, in *Orpheus Descending, A Streetcar Named Desire* and *Death of a Salesman* Miller and Williams present an intellectually, spiritually and morally diminished world where 'mini-martyrs' wage their battles and stage their sacrifices, often to failed ideals.

4

Self-reflection as Heroism

For some playwrights, in an age of ethical relativism and aesthetic fragmentation, dramatic explorations and re-definitions of heroism fulfill a perceived need for a unifying moral vision and provide a semblance of an uninterrupted dramatic tradition. The playwrights who have tried to keep tragedy alive seem to believe that as long as significant action in modern drama can be understood in reference to past ideas of tragedy, the contemporary protagonist can be viewed in terms of heroism. The heroic dedication to idealism need not always be externalized as, for example, in the case of the martyr play. The fateful quest and the concomitant suffering may be internalized, and heroism may take the form of intense self-reflection. For instance, in *Death of a Salesman, A Streetcar Named Desire, Key Largo* and *After the Fall,* to mention four very different plays, the protagonists attempt to discover some value in the midst of meaninglessness and, in some cases, end by dedicating themselves to this fateful challenge. Although their sacrifice to their idealism does not necessarily follow any traditional (that is, classical or Shakespearean) pattern or have the expected repercussions, it is heroic in its intensity.

In the two Miller plays, in the Williams play, and also in his *The Glass Menagerie,* the quest for meaning is fuelled by a need to reconstruct a previously shattered personal vision and reestablish familial and social ties. For instance, Willy Loman's or Blanche DuBois' self-destruction is not only a protest against the prevailing system, but also – and perhaps more significantly – a dedicated, if failed, attempt to reconstitute a disintegrating psyche as well as to re-enter a society from which he or she has been exiled. Keeping with the romanticism of a number of the plays, for the protagonist, the recreation of the self and reestablishment of a relationship with the external world usually involve the process of self-reflection, self-judgement and self-justification; therefore, the reconstitution of reality and redefinition of character require a predominantly subjective dramatic approach.

It is a truism that the pluralism and ethical relativism of the modern era are in part responsible for the increasing subjectivism in drama. That is, social alienation – the cause as well as the result of the subjectivism – has been echoed in the intensified inwardness of a segment of modern theatre. The relationship between this alienation and inwardness is reciprocal: the more the protagonists are viewed as victims of an inimical and overpowering social environment, the more intense their spiritual anguish; the more self-reflective they become, the greater and more total their alienation, and yet the more focused their desire to re-enter the alienating environment. For instance, the more Blanche is made to feel an intruder by an increasingly hostile world, the more she must depend 'on the kindness of strangers'; and the more she depends on their kindness, the stranger and the more alienating they become. Indeed, both Willy Loman and Blanche DuBois are torn between the necessity to remain outsiders and the desire to be a part of a larger community.

They are doomed to remain outsiders by virtue not only of their heightened sensitivity to social injustices and societal hypocrisies and of their refusal to accept these without at least private protest, but also, and equally importantly, as a result of their acute awareness of their own moral transgressions. However, their resulting alienation and withdrawal into the world of their guilty conscience causes them such anguish that it engenders an equally strong desire to reintegrate into the community. This internalized conflict between separation and integration provides the intensity in these plays and in the end completely overwhelms and destroys the protagonists. The willingness to undergo it, at all cost, indicates the characters' fateful dedication.

The protagonist's quest for a comprehensive vision of the world may be a synthesizing process which may have an integrating function and a liberating effect, as it does for Quentin in *After the Fall* and for Tom in *The Glass Menagerie*. In the Miller play, the protagonist progresses from a sense of confusion about his life and a loss of faith, couched in terms of existential anguish, to an integral vision through a mental reenactment of and a reconciliation to past actions. Similarly, Tom Wingfield, in *The Glass Menagerie*, engages in a dramatic recreation of scenes from his oppressive family life and attempts to come to terms with his guilt for having escaped the trap. The journeys of self-exploration and self-judgement lead to spiritual renewal for Quentin and Tom. Although there is an indication of a continual return to this process of self-examination/reconciliation – especially in *The Glass Menagerie* where the melancholy tone at the end of the play ushers in a climate of regret and guilt – the cycle is complete within each play when the reconciliation is accomplished.

The integrating impulse may also have destructive consequences, as it does in *Death of a Salesman* and *A Streetcar Named Desire* where the protagonists embark on a journey toward disintegration and self-destruction – mental in the case of Blanche, physical in the case of Willy. These characters are unable to complete the reconciliating cycle. In the course of the journey they become alienated from themselves and are able to reappropriate their identity only in death, whether of the spirit or of the body. What distinguishes the protagonists of *After the Fall* and *The Glass Menagerie* from those of *A Streetcar Named Desire* and *Death of a Salesman* is that whereas the former conduct a highly conscious, deliberate self-examination through a controlled mental re-enactment of the past, the latter are driven by external circumstances and by their own impending madness to destructive self-absorption.

Therefore, subjectivism may be destructive or creative (involuntary or deliberate) depending on the extent to which the protagonist is able to transcend the initial self-absorption and return to an objective, externalizing view of the world. If, like the protagonist of *Death of a Salesman,* he or she is overwhelmed by the subjective vision, the result will be self-annihilating. If, however, the protagonist's self-examination takes the form of conscious self-dramatization, as in *The Glass Menagerie,* or of intellectualized self-analysis, as in *After the Fall,* the integrating propensities of the subjective journey will dominate and give direction to the quest. In other words, self-reflection may be destructive unless transcended by means of an act of imagination that deconstructs and reconstructs rather than destroys and annihilates. For either type of protagonist the heroic intensity of the experience resides not in the actions taken but in the anguished self-reflection.

John Gassner is one of a number of critics who equate tragic stature with self-consciousness. He states in 'Tragedy in the Modern Theatre' that the 'very elevation or "stature" we have considered essential to the characters of high tragedy is an elevation of intellect – that is, of spirit made supremely conscious of itself by suffering' (54). Thus he equates not only stature with self-consciousness, but also self-consciousness with suffering. Furthermore, the end of any tragedy is enlightenment, precipitated by 'some inherent, cumulatively achieved understanding, realization, or recognition' (52). Gassner believes that this important aspect of tragedy has to do with an objectification of the subjective, or an externalization of individual internalized sentiment. It is precisely this objectification that Willy is unable to achieve. In *Death of a Salesman* and in *A Streetcar Named Desire* reconciliation is partial and comes too late, by the time both Willy and Blanche have reached a point of no return. For them, the external world gradually slips away as their identities are destroyed; by contrast, for Tom Wingfield and for Quentin it is made whole and meaningful at the end of the dramatized – and thus externalized – internal quest.

It may be appropriate at this point to recall George Lukács's ideas on internalization of conflicts in modern drama because his analysis of the interplay between alienation and inwardness is relevant to the plays discussed here. In reference to nineteenth-century German dramatists, and in particular to Hebbel's equation of suffering with action, Lukács contends in his 1909 study on 'The Sociology of Modern Drama' that:

> The heroes of the new drama – in comparison to the old – are more passive than active; they are acted upon more than they act for themselves; they defend rather then attack; their heroism is mostly a heroism of anguish, of despair, not one of bold aggressiveness. Since so much of the inner man has fallen prey to destiny, the last battle is to be enacted within. We can best summarize by saying that the more the vital motivating centre is displaced outward (i.e., the greater the determining force of external factors), the more the centre of tragic conflict is drawn inward; it becomes internalized, more exclusively a conflict in the spirit. For up to a certain limit, the inner powers of resistance upon which the spirit can depend become greater and more intense in direct proportion to the greatness and intensity of the outwardly opposing forces. (Bentley, 1976, 429)

This analysis is applicable to figures like Willy, Blanche, Val Xavier and Brick, for instance, who seldom stage an attack; at best they react, often by refusing to act, by demonstrating their unwillingness to behave in a manner expected of them. Their protest is often silent and ineffectual, as in the case of Brick or Willy. Nonetheless, their soundless outcry is an apt metaphor for their isolated mental suffering.

In *Death of a Salesman,* a dramatization of a private response to the social climate, Miller explores an alienation/inwardness relationship such as the one described by Lukács. Lukács points out that the external assault on the protagonists results in their internalization of the conflict. That is, the protagonists come to embody the two irreconcilable imperatives operating in the external world: for example, Willy is both a staunch supporter of the competitive system and its pathetic casualty. His mutually exclusive allegiances contribute to his psychic disintegration. Furthermore, the more deterministic the external environment, the more crushing the sense of fate and the greater the protagonist's internalization of suffering; as Willy is both controlled by the deterministic social forces and estranged from his social environment, he becomes self-reflective and self-enclosed.

The alienation/inwardness relationship constitutes both the form and the theme of the play. Miller shows the protagonist at that point in his life when he has internalized the conflict between two aspects of American liberalism – individual integrity and capitalist utilitarianism – and has become totally self-absorbed as a result of his alienation. It is as a consequence of the alienating socio-political system and of deterministic economic conditions that Willy Loman feels more at home in the world of his imagination than in his actual environment, whether in his house, at work, or on the road.

The fact that he is overwhelmed by his inner world may be seen as constituting a critique of the external world; that is, as a result, at least in part, of his estrangement from an environment which no longer has any use for him, Willy has in effect been forced to retreat into a world of his own creation where the conflicts are now enacted. The more he retreats into this private world, the less capable he is of functioning within his 'real' environment. The more he is objectified by the outside world, the more subjective he becomes. His self-imposed exile from reality, his mental disintegration and his solipsism are a result of his extreme reaction to social and private circumstances which may affect all members of that society but which affect Willy fatally.

Like most modern protagonists, Willy is representative of large sections of humanity, but it is his excessive response to his fate that marks him as a hero. The response may be excessive in terms of societal expectations and norms, but the point is that in an ideal world – which the playwright, together with the audience, suggestively delineates through his rejection of the fallen world – it is entirely appropriate and necessary. Through the dramatization of an intensified response, of an extreme reaction to ordinary circumstances, Miller elevates the commonplace – the unquestioned and unexamined – realities of life to a dramatic and conceptual level where they cannot but undergo close scrutiny. The victimization of self-deluded Willy Lomans continues largely unnoticed. But when the protagonist Willy Loman, in an embodiment of the system's ideology, is finally martyred to his own idealized understanding in such a manner that his very death becomes the death of all salesmen and of all those who sell their soul for profit, Miller believes 'attention must be paid'.

Miller explains in his 'Introduction to the Collected Plays' that he wanted

> to make a play with the veritable countenance of life. To make one the many, as in life, so that 'society' is a power and a mystery of custom and inside the man and surrounding him, as the fish is in the sea and the sea inside the fish, his birthplace and burial ground, promise and threat. (30)

As Miller understands the interdependent relationship between individual and society, the individual both forms society and is formed by it. Therefore the fate of the seemingly insignificant individual must be the fate of the society, and society's conflicts must be the individual's conflicts. When individuals try to segregate themselves from society or are unwittingly alienated from that society which constitutes an integral part of them, the consequences must be severe.

Willy's individual fate may have no direct bearing on society – it in no way disturbs the order – but his whole life, and especially his death, is emblematic of the prevalent materialistic ideology. In this sense, Willy's tragedy is really society's tragedy, since his fate is neither private nor isolated. Paradoxically, in the end Willy believes that he has gained social acceptance – if not for himself, at least for his sons – by giving up his existence. He commits suicide for the life insurance and thus sells himself in order to buy Biff's way to success. In this sense, it is Willy's death rather than his life that aptly exemplifies materialistic society, for it is his one profitable act of salesmanship. Selling, a way of life, here becomes a way of death. Miller, who when asked what it was that Willy was in fact selling replied 'himself', seems to believe that the person who lives by selling must die by selling. Indeed, it is appropriate that Willy, who dreams of the serene death and beautiful funeral of the travelling salesman Dave Singleman, should die a violent death and have an undistinguished, uneventful funeral attended by a few bewildered mourners.

All this is not to say that Willy is merely a puppet of his external environment or that he has completely appropriated its characteristics. He is as much a victim of his own delusions and misconceptions as of societal values. Of course, one could argue that his delusions are not his own but are a product of societal propaganda. No doubt, Willy is driven by a combination of factors. Even the cause of his suicide is not clearly identifiable, says Miller, but rather is 'so mixed in motive as to be unfathomable'. According to the playwright, there was 'revenge . . . in it and a power of love, a victory in that it would bequeath a fortune to the living and a flight from emptiness' ('Introduction to the Collected Plays', 30). And, one may add, it is an act of cowardice and of bravery, of a fatal clarity of vision and a fatal lack of vision. It is a modern equivalent of sorts to the Faustian bargain with the Devil (rather than for knowledge, Willy bargains for money and for his son's love); in the end Willy is seduced by Ben's voice of success into killing himself. His suicide may mark a refusal to live a life of alienation but it is also a final submission to and glorification of the system's alienating values. By killing himself, Willy commits the final act of self-alienation.

The suicide – foreshadowed at the beginning of the play – follows the final showdown between Biff and Willy, where the son's attack centres on his father's delusions and culminates in Willy's recollected scene about his son's discovery of the father's sexual infidelity. Biff, shattered by this confrontation with his father, relinquishes all ambitions in life. Willy's suicide is in part an act of penance for the betrayal of his son and a payment for Biff's lost youth.

During the play's last confrontation between father and son, Biff, no longer able to contain his fury, deflates Willy's ego when he tells him: 'I am not a leader of men, Willy, and neither are you. You were never anything but a hard-working drummer who landed in the ash can like all the rest of them! I'm one dollar an hour, Willy!' (217). He accuses his father of being a failure and failing to recognize the fact. And it is this final attack in the present that brings about not only a moment of filial reconciliation (father and son realize that they love each other) but also Willy's decision to sacrifice his life for his son's future by selling his own life for the insurance money. For Willy, death is a release of sorts from the bondage of success.

Causation in the play is complicated by a very specific aspect of Willy's inwardness: his feelings of guilt concerning his infidelity or more precisely, the betrayal of his sons. Despite Linda's memorable presence, *Death of a Salesman* is very much a men's play, as are Miller's other plays. The father–son relationship, rather than the one between husband and wife, forms the core of the play. It is not to his wife but to his son that the father feels the need to apologize, and it is that trust that has been breached, not the marital one. The central theme is the shattering of illusions, not sexual infidelity; Willy knows that he is not what or who he built himself up to be and therefore fears nothing more than to be abandoned by his boys, and it is when they leave him in the restaurant and walk away with the women they had just met that Willy re-lives his most painful confrontation with his son – when he betrayed Biff, and Biff in turn betrayed him, when he 'cut down [his] life for spite' (215). Linda may speak for Willy, champion his cause, be his confidante, but it is Biff's resentment that torments Willy throughout his recollections. Willy's suicide is an attempt to give back to Biff his youthful hope and the financial means with which to realize his dreams. Of course, Willy also recognizes that Biff is a younger version of himself and that his life will continue in Biff.

In this play, as in *The Crucible,* the protagonist's feeling of culpability has to do not with the 'crime' (witchcraft in one play, financial failure in the other) for which, according to his society, he is paying his due but with betrayal in the form of adultery. According to moral arbiters external to the play – that is, the playwright and the audience – Willy is punished for his adherence to false values, but even this judgement seems to be overshadowed by the theme of adultery. Miller's penchant for equating societal betrayal and private betrayal, the latter often presented in the form of sexual infidelity, results not only in an interesting mélange of motives but at times also in a confusion of ideas. This is particularly evident in *After the Fall* where Miller has Quentin in his stream-of-consciousness recollection create an odd mix of all of life's turmoils – from Nazi atrocities and Cold War purges to marital difficulties and psychological problems – and lay indiscriminate blame on all of humanity for the war crimes against humanity. The play's lack of political and historical awareness is a factor not so much of Miller's insensitivity but of an occasionally awkward attempt to illustrate the interrelation of private and public life. One may argue that this makes for more complex drama, for causation is seldom of one source; however, the fact that adultery lurks in the background of *Death of a Salesman* and of *The Crucible*, plays which ostensibly have very little to do with marital fidelity or with sexual matters, also makes for a less sharply defined conflict.

Thus Proctor's self-sacrificing impulse, as we have seen, is as much a product of his feelings of sinfulness as of his dedication to a cause. Similarly, what – dramatically speaking – finally drives Willy to suicide is not his lack of success as a salesman or his disillusionment with the system, but the knowledge that his marital disloyalty was the cause of Biff's disenchantment and resulting lack of ambition and that he had failed as a father. In both plays, the issue of adultery occupies a central position and clouds the actual subject, which in the case of *The Crucible* has to do with the mass hysteria and public persecution surrounding political purges, and in *Death of a Salesman* with the self-destruction of one of the system's faithful but unsuccessful servants.

Awareness of Miller's preoccupation in these plays with adultery, and later in *After the Fall* with original sin, may help clarify why he refers to Willy's dramatised interior monologue as a confession. In his 'Introduction to the Collected Plays' he comments that the play seems to take

> the form of a confession, for that is how it is told, now speaking of what happened yesterday, then suddenly following some connection to a time twenty years ago, then leaping even further back and then returning to the present and even speculating about the future. (24)

It is doubtful whether this is an adequate description of a confession – Miller seems to be describing a recollection; however, the fact that he sees the play in these terms is a significant indication of the role he assigns to guilt in recollections and perhaps even of the quasi-religious function he finds in self-reflection. Although there is a temptation to compare the 'confessional' structure of *Death of a Salesman* to that of *After the Fall*, the protagonist in the former cannot reasonably be conceived as having undertaken a confession, for his admission of guilt is not always conscious or deliberate.

Like Blanche, Willy reveals a great deal about himself and may even repent – if regret concerning his past actions can be equated with repentance – but he is not in fact confessing. In the case of Willy, the necessary interplay between introspection and analysis is missing. He is neither analytical enough nor distanced enough from his own despair to be capable of genuine self-analysis. Furthermore, there is no confessor in the play, not even in the form of an unidentified 'listener' such as one finds in *After the Fall*. The fact that Willy is unable to transcend total self-absorption through self-analysis is one factor in his tragic disintegration.

Due to the necessary subjectivism of *Death of a Salesman*, Miller articulated, from the earliest conception of the play, the idea of a simultaneity of events reflecting the character's consciousness:

> The image was in direct opposition to the method of *All My Sons* – a method one might call linear or eventual in that one fact or incident creates the necessity for the next. The *Salesman* image was from the beginning absorbed with the concept that nothing in life comes 'next' but that everything exists together and at the same time within us; that there is no past to be 'brought forward' in a human being, but that he is his past at every moment and that the present is merely that which his past is capable of noticing and smelling and reacting to. ('Introduction to the Collected Plays', 23)

The concept of the play, Miller recalled later, grew out of a series of 'structural images', (30) the first being that 'of an enormous face the height of the proscenium arch which would appear and then open up, and we would see the inside of a man's head' (23). Miller felt that he wanted 'to create a form which, in itself as a form, would literally be the process of Willy Loman's way of mind' (23–4). In other words, rather than an objective description of Willy's thought process, it would be the subjective thought process itself.

Miller uses the stream-of-consciousness technique, with its potential for simultaneous exploration of past and present, to show a man discarded by a utilitarian society and drawn increasingly deeper into and finally irretrievably lost to his subjective, alienated world. Comparing the form of *Death of a Salesman* with that of *All My Sons*, Miller explains, in reference to the former, that

> What was wanted now was not a mounting line of tension, nor a gradually narrowing cone of intensifying suspense, but a bloc, a

> single chord presented as such at the outset, within which all the strains and melodies would already be contained. ('Introduction to the Collected Plays', 24)

He describes the play in terms of a unified image beyond time, as a series of dramatized moments of consciousness, rather than as a temporally defined linear structure. In resorting to what he calls expressionistic elements, Miller feels that he is employing a technique that the audience might perhaps consider to be excessively objective and therefore alienating. In the 'Introduction to the Collected Plays', he explains that the play's

> expressionistic elements were consciously used as such, but since the approach to Willy Loman's characterization was consistently and rigorously subjective, the audience would not ever be aware – if I could help it – that they were witnessing the use of a technique which had until then created only coldness, objectivity, and a highly styled sort of play. I had willingly employed expressionism but always to create a subjective truth . . . (39)

Miller shares O'Neill's ambivalence toward German theatrical expressionism,[1] but believes that he can use expressionism for his own specific purposes:

> I had always been attracted and repelled by the brilliance of German expressionism after World War I, and one aim in *Salesman* was to employ its quite marvelous shorthand for humane, 'felt' characterizations rather than for the purposes of demonstration for which the Germans had used it. ('Introduction to the Collected Plays', 39)

The stylizing, objectifying and depersonalizing tendencies of German theatrical expressionism seem to go counter Miller's, and a number of other American playwrights' preference for realism and psychological character analysis. However, what Miller calls 'felt' characterization was widely used by German expressionist painters, and it is this type of expressionism, which finds painterly equivalents for subjective states of mind, rather than that of the German theatre, that perhaps most closely approximates Miller's and O'Neill's subjectifying version of expressionism.

A large part of the play's action is a recreation of Willy's mental processes and, in fact, as Brian Parker indicates in 'Point of View in *Death of a Salesman*' (Corrigan 95–105) Willy's point of view dominates the play to a degree that even those scenes where he does not appear (for example the 'Requiem') are seen from his vantage point. It is at the point where the subjective consciousness clashes with the objective reality that the conflict occurs. Parker observes that the values of the play are limited to whatever Willy's own imagination can discern and therefore suggests that Miller's technique is reminiscent of the morality play, for the various characters are voices of Willy's conscience. This is a useful comparison; however, while from a technical point of view, Willy's consciousness seems, as Parker asserts, to dominate the play, there is another form of reality operating here. Miller brings to a crisis the confrontation between 'a mounting line of tension' – the external conflict between Willy and his employer, between Willy and Biff – and 'a mobile concurrency of past and present' – Willy's internalized conflict between memory and reality ('Introduction to the Collected Plays' 26). Or, in other words, he shows a battle between fate (a function of external factors) and the war within the self. This clash of two ultimately irreconcilable forces internalized by a disintegrating figure, rather than a quarrel among Willy's diverse voices of conscience, best characterizes the central conflicts in the play. The play's effectiveness and originality resides precisely in this dramatization of a linear, Aristotelian dramatic structure confronting a subjective, contemplative view of reality.

For Willy, self-reflection brings partial reconciliation, but the price he pays is total estrangement from objective reality. Similarly, Blanche's confession to Mitch frees her of her burden of guilt, but it further alienates her from the present. In both plays introspection and self-trial for past transgressions bring only limited enlightenment because the protagonists are destroyed in the confrontation with reality; their clashes with the external world lead to insanity or death. Willy and Blanche embark on painful journeys toward social reintegration and end their journeys as outsiders. They are not able to transcend their inwardness; their suffering is not objectified through imagination because their self-reflection, or rather self-absorption, is often involuntary.

Indeed, Willy's introspection constitutes his demise. Miller has commented in the 'Introduction to the Collected Plays' on the determinism of the play and on his own awareness, as Willy's creator, of the inevitability of Willy's journey toward death:

> The play was begun with one firm piece of knowledge and this was that Loman was to destroy himself. How it would wander before it got to that point I did not know and resolved not to care. I was convinced only that if I could make him remember enough he would kill himself, and the structure of the play was determined by what was needed to draw up his memories like a mass of tangled root without end or beginning. (25)

Thus Willy cannot avoid death; his complete submission to self-reflection in the course of his quest for forgiveness acquires the characteristics of fate. Indeed, one could say that he is *driven* instead of just *dedicated*.

His long and arduous process of remembrance is motivated partly by the desire to return to a time of innocence, a time before choice. Willy, Blanche, Tom Wingfield and Quentin repeatedly return to the crucial moments of their past, when they had made their fateful decisions, and recollect the special moments of innocence. Willy's self-exploration takes him back to the boys' childhood and to a period that, Willy believes, was one of America's innocence and naívete. In these moments of retrogression he can still dream of success. Similarly, Blanche recalls her life at the plantation Belle Reve before Alan Grey's suicide.

The escape into the past represents a flight from unbearable actuality into possibility because in a world without future, all hope and potential lies in recreating the past to suit one's needs. As Mary Tyrone (in *Long Day's Journey into Night*) observes, the future is always determined by the past, and thus no one in the present has control over it. However, the past exists only in the memory and is accessible through the imagination. Thus, ironically enough, the past is open to interpretation; on the other hand, in this scheme of things the future is time-bound, already fixed because it is predetermined.

Quentin, in *After the Fall*, is at pains to bring back a time of personal and political innocence. In the 'Foreword to *After the Fall*' Miller observes that

> through Quentin's agony in this play there runs the everlasting temptation of Innocence, that deep desire to return to when, it seems, he was in fact without blame. To that elusive time, which persists in all our minds, when somehow everything was part of us and we so pleasurably at one with others, and everything

> merely 'happened' to us. But the closer he examines those seemingly unified years the clearer it becomes that his Paradise keeps slipping back and back. (256–7)

In his quest for innocence, Quentin comes face to face with all his past choices, with 'the conflict between his own needs and desires and the impediments others put in his way', and finally with his own guilt. Typically, in this play, as well as in a number of others, out of the desire for innocence comes the confrontation with guilt.

Miller and Williams dramatize not only the alienation of their protagonists but also their tragic attempt at re-familiarization. Indeed, contrary to the expectations one might have about tragic alienation, a play such as *A Streetcar Named Desire*, for instance, shows an already alienated protagonist attempting to reintegrate into society. The desire for reintegration is often inseparable from the yearning for a return to an innocent past. The playwrights', and therefore their protagonists', relationship to the past partakes of an ambivalence: Willy, Blanche, Quentin and Tom Wingfield are simultaneously drawn to the past and repelled by it. The past constitutes not only the source of their fate but is also that already familiar, if somewhat haunting, territory where they think they can escape from a threatening present and an uncertain future. However, this escape into the past often has disastrous consequences because it implies a potentially fatal confrontation with guilt. As a result of their character, the heroic protagonists are fated to embark on a self-reflective quest which inevitably leads them to this confrontation.

In order to transcend self-consciousness, the playwright – and within the play, the protagonist in *The Glass Menagerie* and in *After the Fall* – deliberately dramatizes the process of consciousness and exposes it to critical scrutiny. It is precisely this intellectualizing quality and the resulting aesthetic distance conferred on reality through the analytical nature of the dramatization that help objectify the subjective experience and thus transcend self-consciousness through flights of imagination.

In light of Miller's subjectivism in *Death of a Salesman* and of his increasing tendencies in that direction, it is noteworthy that in his essays on the theatre he waged a long battle against dramatic subjectivism, in particular against what he saw as a new romanticism. In a 1960 interview he describes the fifties as 'an era of gauze' for which, he believes, 'Tennessee Williams is responsible . . . in the main'. However, he admits to partial guilt, when he confesses that 'One of . . . [his] own feet stands in this stream'. He maintains that to remedy this 'cruel, romantic neuroticism, a translation of current life into the war within the self' playwrights will have to dramatize fate, 'the world beyond the skin'. (*The Theater Essays*, 232). Even though there is an attempt in *Death of a Salesman* to describe 'the world beyond the skin' – the social and economic conditions that created Willy – 'the war within the self' is the primary force in the play; the world beyond the skin has been absorbed by a thin-skinned Willy. Moreover, Willy's character and his idiosyncrasies constitute his fate to no lesser degree than Brick's or Blanche's do.

Espousing an anti-psychological view in the fifties, Miller repeatedly blames the perceived irreconcilability of the individual's private desire and public role on the perpetuation of asocial attitudes in life and on the stage and calls for a return to 'social drama' which would show the individual and society in a reciprocal and interdependent relationship. Criticizing the play of exclusive psychological motivation, he argues that 'it is no longer possible to contain the truth of the human situation so totally within a single man's guts as the bulk of our plays presuppose', and announces his intention to emphasize ultimate causes rather than mere effects ('Brewed in *The Crucible*', 172).

In the 'Introduction to the Collected Plays' he argues that for modern drama to be faithful to reality it must reflect and dramatize the mutually dependent relationship between the individual and the society. Miller also maintains that by dramatizing the protagonist's attempt to reintegrate into and survive in society, rather than focusing only on the asocial, self-enclosed individual, the playwright can explore the relationship between individual and society and also the tension between a person's private and public identities. Many of Miller's alienated outsiders – Willy, Proctor, Quentin – struggle to retain their integrity and establish their private, non-public identity; they also, however, desperately struggle to rejoin the public realm.

Throughout *The Theater Essays*, Miller contends that he has tried to explore both private and public life and to achieve a balance between the protagonist's internal conflict and his or her conflict with the external world. However, his insistence in the essays on the necessity and desirability of dramatizing the interrelationship between individual and social reality is not a reliable indicator of his much more problematic practice and specifically of his increasing subjectivism. In fact, his relationship to 'social drama' as he defines it in a number of his essays, and in 'The Social Play' and 'Introduction to the Collected Plays' in particular, is much more complex than he would have one believe. In the article 'Brewed in *The Crucible*' he asserts that:

> Analytical psychology, when so intensely exploited as to reduce the world to the size of a man's abdomen and to equate his fate with his neurosis, is a reemergence of romanticism. It is inclined to deny all outer forces until man is only his complex. It presupposes an autonomy in the human character that, in a word, is false. A neurosis is not a fate but an effect. (174)

And yet, his own plays, even the early *All My Sons*, display a propensity for psychologizing and for extreme subjectivism. Willy's fate certainly cannot be equated with his neurosis; however, his character traits are major contributing factors to his demise, and the conflict between objective reality and Willy's subjective vision is couched in personal terms and dramatized in an entirely subjective manner. Although Miller does delineate an external world, there is no acceptable external corrective to Willy's vision.

Clearly, already in *Death of a Salesman* there are indications of the new direction Miller's playwriting takes in *After the Fall*. The self-reflective inwardness of that play, what Miller considers the 'confessional' structure and the reliance on formal, theatrical equivalents of mental processes find early expression in *Death of a Salesman*. By the time he writes *After the Fall* (1964), after a nine-year hiatus during the McCarthy era, he seems to have abandoned his understanding of evil as a product of remediable social and political contingencies. In an ideological about-face, he now posits evil not in society or in political systems but in invariably sinful human nature. As a consequence, Miller considers *After the Fall* as

> a way of looking at man and his human nature as the only source of the violence which has come closer and closer to destroying the race. It is a view which does not look toward social or political ideas as the creators of violence but into the nature of the human being himself. ('Foreword to *After the Fall*', 255)

Although historical events and social realities play a key role in this play, the focus is not social, at least not directly. In this play the author distances the action from objective, external reality when he situates it entirely within the mind of his central character. Self-consciousness, self-analysis and the resulting internalized conflicts constitute the action in this play and denote a quest for meaning.

Miller is preoccupied with legal and moral transgression and with trial, judgement and punishment and considers a play 'a series of jurisprudence' where 'some part . . . must take the advocate's role, something else must act in defense, and the entirety must engage the Law' ('Introduction to the Collected Plays', 24–5). Several of his plays contain a real or figurative condemnation and trial of the protagonist either by a member of his family – *All My Sons, Death of a Salesman* – or by society – *The Crucible, A View from the Bridge* and indirectly *Death of a Salesman.* In *All My Sons* the father is forced by the son to admit his guilt. Similarly, Willy drives himself to suicide through his destructive self-reflection which is fuelled by his guilt feelings regarding his son. Proctor in *The Crucible,* on the other hand, is a victim of persecution by the community and a tortured penitent haunted by his own sense of sin. It is the lawyer Quentin, the protagonist of *After the Fall,* who is the most acutely conscious and self-conscious of Miller's protagonists.

What passes for self-destruction and madness in *Death of a Salesman* and in *A Streetcar Named Desire* constitutes a creative and liberating act for Tom in *The Glass Menagerie* and for Quentin in *After the Fall.* Acting as self-dramatizing authors of their own past and creators of their destinies, these two protagonists transform guilt-ridden memory into art – through a confessional re-enactment of their past rivaling in intensity the heroism of external action – and thus achieve a kind of reconciliation and enlightenment of which neither Blanche nor Willy is capable. *The Glass Menagerie* and *After the Fall* are not plays *about* reconciliation, they *are* rituals of reconciliation.

Like *All My Sons, After the Fall* is also concerned with complicity and with universal brotherhood. Contemplating the horror of the concentration camps, Quentin exclaims: 'My brothers died here . . . but my brothers built this place; our hearts have cut these stones!' (241) Unlike earlier plays, however, this play emphasizes guilt rather than responsibility, passive self-analysis rather than action; in *After the Fall* Miller shows individuals and the social group as inherently guilty (as a result of having the power to choose evil) but also equipped with the capacity to love and to forgive.

The main source of anguish for Quentin at the beginning of the play is the realization that he may be a guilty man but that there is no one to judge him. The play begins with a painful recognition, not unlike that of existentialist despair, as Quentin recalls his first awareness of emptiness. Perhaps because he is a lawyer, he sees life in legal terms:

> A life, after all, is evidence . . . for many years I looked at life like a case at law, a series of proofs . . . But underlying it all, I see now, there was a presumption. That I was moving on an upward path toward some elevation, where – God knows what – I would be justified, or even condemned – a verdict anyway. I think now that my disaster really began when I looked up one day – and the bench was empty. No judge in sight. (129)

With this existential revelation of total abandonment begins Quentin's journey of self-examination and his quest for meaning. A representative of guilty humanity, of individual and society after the fall, Quentin is more than a product of society; he is its conscience.

The play explores, instead of an individual's conflict with society, one person's coming to terms with his own perceptions of existence at a point far removed from the state of innocence, in terms of his personal history and the history of humanity. Miller believes that humanity's fall from innocence is signalled by 'the fall from non-conscious existence'; in turn, the fall into consciousness is accompanied by the 'threat of freedom' ('The Will to Live' 356). The anguished discovery of nothingness and the inheritance of freedom entail internal struggle and intense mental and emotional anguish. Quentin's thought processes, his tortured attempt to deal with his and others' guilt and to return to innocence, constitute the action of the play. Whereas Tom Wingfield recreates representative moments in his past in the form of a play, Quentin recalls the crucial moments in his life as a dramatized series of confrontations between various people.

He is about to meet a woman who would mean a new life for him. Faced with this event, he reviews his past, his private life and his public role, against the backdrop of recent history. As the *dramatis personae* of his past come to life in his imagination and on stage, Quentin analyses his two failed marriages, the beginnings of a new relationship with the woman he is about to meet, his childhood during the Depression, as well as his professional experiences during the McCarthy era. Unlike Williams in *The Glass Menagerie,* who shows his protagonist transforming self-consciousness into a highly structured art form and posing as narrator/stage director, Miller dramatizes Quentin's pre-verbal stage of consciousness.

In *After the Fall* there is no conflict between realism/objective time and expressionism/subjective time as there is in *Death of a Salesman*; here we are entirely in the landscape of the mind. Miller tries to establish stage equivalents for this mental locale:

> *The setting consists of three levels rising to the highest at the back, crossing in a curve from one side of the stage to the other . . . On the two lower levels are sculpted areas; indeed, the whole effect is neolithic, a lava-like, supple geography in which, like pits and hollows found in lava, the scenes take place. The mind has no color but its memories are brilliant against the grayness of its landscape . . . People appear and disappear instantaneously, as in the mind . . . The effect, therefore, will be the surging, flitting, instantaneousness of a mind questing over its own surface and into its depths.* (127)

The most menacing element, completely dominating the stage, is the blasted stone tower of a German concentration camp which rises above the three levels. Its windows are *'like eyes which at the moment seem blind and dark; bent reinforcing rods stick out of it like broken tentacles'* (127). Miller commented in an interview that he used the camp in the play as 'the final expression of human separateness and its ultimate consequence. It is organized abandonment . . . one of the prime themes of *After the Fall*' ('The Will to Live', 356)

Betrayal on all levels and in all its forms constitutes the play's leitmotif. Quentin repeatedly recalls those scenes where he was betrayed or where he betrayed others. Because in memory all events can have equal psychological value, Miller is at liberty to draw the ideologically and morally suspect parallel between betrayal and guilt on the private level and on the public level. Thus when Quentin's memory conjures up instances of individual treachery, the camp's tower lights up. Quentin's first betrayal by his parents (their going to Atlantic city without telling him) is given not only the same psychological weight, but also the same moral value as one man's betrayal of his colleague at a hearing of the committee on un-American activities, or the omnipresent horrors of the concentration camp. Similarly, visions of his wife's suicide are juxtaposed with those of the German camps. Such simplistic equating of public and private acts, facilitated by the stream-of-consciousness technique, precludes a serious political or historical reading of the play.

Quentin's awareness of the meaninglessness of existence is akin to the nausea Raquentin experiences in Sartre's *La Nausée*. Miller has remarked that he shares Sartre's views concerning freedom, choice and responsibility ('The Will to Live'). Such statements, as well as certain elements in the later plays, particularly in *After the Fall*, have encouraged critical identification of Miller with the existentialists, despite his denial of any direct influence. However, an obvious similarity exists between Miller's play and Camus' *La Chute* (1956, trans. *The Fall*, 1957). In this novella, Clamence – a lawyer, like Quentin – examines his life and his beliefs as he confesses to a reader/listener and comes to the conclusion that 'since we are all judges, we are all guilty before one another, all Christs in our mean manner, one by one crucified, always without knowing' (116–17). Like Quentin, he recognizes the horror of being without a judge and yet being fated to judge oneself:

> He who clings to a law does not fear the judgment that reinstates him in an order he believes in. But the keenest of human torments is to be judged without a law. Yet we are in that torment. (117)

Although it is not always so clearly articulated, the awareness of lawlessness or godlessness torments many of the protagonists in the plays under discussion. The pluralism of the modern world and the supposed lack of any clearly discernible overriding moral order are manifestation of the same phenomenon. Whereas traditional protagonists were often condemned like criminals for their transgressions, modern protagonists are often shown as uncondemned criminals having to take the stand in a court of justice presided over by their own conscience. This seems to be the fate of such diverse protagonists as Quentin, Willy, Blanche, Mary Tyrone, Larry Slade and Don Parritt. These characters are condemned to freedom, to self-consciousness and to destructive feelings of guilt.

While Quentin's painful cognizance may be existentialistic, the play, not unlike a number of Miller's other plays, makes certain assumptions about the inherent sinfulness of human nature and is concerned more with exploring this kind of determinism than with analyzing the human condition. In this play heroism is to be located not in the tough optimism of the existentialists according to whom the condemnation to freedom implies total personal as well as social responsibility, but rather in the acceptance of guilt and in the ability to overcome its crippling effect.

Quentin must transcend the sense of absurdity which has infected his mind. Although he admits in Act One that 'it seeps in my room, the world, my life, and its pointlessness', he still harbors some hope that he might be free of these feelings if he could only 'corner that hope, find what it consists of, and either kill it for a lie, or really make it mine' (130). He feels that if he can appropriate hope, he can begin living again. To achieve this reconciliation, Quentin must answer for all the public betrayals he has witnessed and even for those from which he has had the fortune to be excluded. As Miller explains in the 'Foreword to *After the Fall*', the play is

> the trial of a man by his own conscience, his own values, his own deeds. The 'listener' who to some will be a psychoanalyst, to others God, is Quentin himself turned at the edge of the abyss to look at his experience, his nature and his time in order to bring to light, to seize and – innocent no more – to forever guard against his own complicity with Cain and the world's. (257)

Quentin's despair leads to his acceptance of sin and of determinism; by contrast, the anguish of freedom, in existentialist thought, culminates in the recognition of choice and in subsequent action. While Quentin must make a choice at the end of the play (whether or not to begin life anew with Holga) the question Miller poses is not whether Quentin is able to define himself, and through himself others, whether in the midst of nothingness he is able to give meaning to existence, but rather whether he can live with the choices he made in the past. Thus the questions posed here and the central conflict dramatized are not that different from those in *Long Day's Journey*, for instance, where the ghosts of the past come to haunt the present and where characters have to survive the consequences of past decisions.

As a result of the moralizing approach of the play, Quentin's progression into knowledge essentially has to do with his acceptance of evil in fallen humanity, and particularly in himself. He laments his loss of innocence as he realizes the perniciousness of even the truth. When his friend Mickey's career is destroyed during the McCarthy era, Quentin despairs:

> So the truth, after all, may merely be murderous? The truth killed Lou; destroyed Mickey. Then what else is there? A workable lie? Maybe there is only one sin, to destroy your own credibility.

> Strength comes from a clear conscience or a dead one. Not to see one's own evil – there's power! And rightness too! So kill conscience. Kill it. (186)

A version of this 'workable lie' is feasible for such protagonists, among others, as Big Daddy in *Cat on a Hot Tin Roof,* who has lived with mendacity all his life, and the occupants of Harry Hope's bar in *The Iceman Cometh,* for whom survival means total surrender to a 'pipe-dream'. Quentin recognizes the 'workable lie' and wishes for a clear or absent conscience; however, knowledge seems to bring with it only greater despair, and innocence is no longer attainable. In the midst of overwhelming freedom, Quentin must be his own judge; he must pass judgement but also exercise clemency because he learns that people must learn to forgive themselves.

Self-forgiveness is what Quentin strives for. His most important discovery is the revelation that hope need not be dependent upon ignorance and innocence. Holga, the Austrian woman Quentin is about to meet, has seen suffering and carries the burden of survivor's guilt. Yet she is able to sustain hope. At the end of the play Quentin has his moment of vision, of insight concerning Holga:

> . . . is that . . . exactly why she hopes, because she knows? What burning cities taught her and the death of love taught me – that we are very dangerous! . . . I swear to you, there's something in me that could dare to love this world again! . . . Is the knowing all? To know, and even happily that we meet unblessed; not in some garden of wax fruit and painted trees, that lie of Eden, but after, after the Fall, after many, many deaths. Is the knowing all? And the wish to kill is never killed, but with some gift of courage one may look into its face when it appears, and with a stroke of love – as to an idiot in the house – forgive it; again and again . . . forever? (241)

Accepting this fallen state and recognizing the power of hatred and his own capacity for evil, Quentin is able to love. Within the world of *After the Fall,* heroism has to do with taking 'one's life in one's arms' (148) and with total acceptance of both individual and collective guilt. The simultaneous acceptance of guilt and transcendence of self-absorption, as well as the consequent breaking of the deadlock, are results of Quentin's intense intellectualization and self-analysis.

Through this imaginative and intellectual process Quentin frees himself of the torment of self-reflection. The anti-realism of the play – particularly its stream-of-consciousness technique – facilitates the dramatization of Quentin's mental processes and ensures a subjective reading of the social and political concerns of the play. That is, the social drama is filtered through the analysing consciousness of the central persona as conflicts are enacted 'inside his head'. As a corrective to the criticism which views Miller solely as a social dramatist and Williams exclusively as a dramatist of personal lyricism, it is useful to call attention to Miller's practice of theatrical subjectivism and to Williams' social concerns, for instance in *The Glass Menagerie*, *The Sweet Bird of Youth* and *Orpheus Descending*.

Unlike Miller, who went through what he has described as an Ibsenite stage, Williams was drawn from the beginning to non-realistic theatrical techniques. In the 'Production Notes' to *The Glass Menagerie* and throughout the stage directions in the play, he voices his plea for anti-realism. He calls for 'a new, plastic theatre which must take the place of the exhausted theatre of realistic conventions if the theatre is to resume vitality as part of our culture' (7). The 'plastic' elements – all the non-verbal elements such as setting, music, lighting, pantomime and other gestural aspects used to emphasize certain thematic elements – constitute a kind of 'objective correlative' for the subjective states of mind. In this play Williams establishes an aesthetic distance through the use of a lyrical narrative, occasionally undercut by irony and analysis, and through various non-textual devices controls the audience's fluctuating empathy.

Williams originally proposed using screens with slogans for 'a definite emotional appeal', in order to accent certain values through ironic legends and other visual devices. The screens were omitted in the original Broadway production but were retained in the Random House edition of the text; consequently, few early commentators mention the screens. This is unfortunate, considering their thematic and formal significance. Because the screens provide frequent ironic commentary on the action, they function as a device which hinders direct audience identification with the characters' emotions. In the 'Production Notes' Williams admits to having felt the need to include them in order to ensure that the audience was not missing the point:

> Each scene contains a particular point (or several) which is structurally the most important. In an episodic play, such as this, the basic structure or narrative time may be obscured from the audience; the effect may be fragmentary rather than architectural. (8)

Presumably, a memory play may take the liberty of being 'fragmentary', yet Williams seems to be worried about the play's formal fragmentation. It would be difficult to determine whether he was well aware of the ironic, metatheatrical function of the screens or whether he actually believed that the screens were needed as signposts, or rather building blocks for an audience used to 'architectural' plots and to the cumulative impact of a Freytagian five act structure. Perhaps he felt the need to provide the necessary punctuation for bewildered critics.

For Williams, as for other playwrights, the ultimate goal in using anti-realistic techniques is the achievement of greater realism. Anti-realism, Williams contends, must have as its aim the presentation of a deeper realism, for 'expressionism and all other unconventional techniques in drama have only one valid aim, and that is a closer approach to truth' ('Production Notes', 7). The play's protagonist echoes this attitude to the relationship between art and life when, as narrator and stage director, he explains:

> Yes, I have tricks in my pockets, I have things up my sleeve. But I am the opposite of a stage magician. He gives you illusion that has the appearance of truth. I give you truth in the pleasant disguise of illusion. (22)

Art parading as reality – illusion disguised as truth – constitutes the most facile form of realism; Williams/Tom Wingfield opts for the deeper realism of reality transformed into art – truth disguised as illusion. If we assume that Tom is here speaking for Williams, and I think we can assume that here, Tom's statement is further evidence of the playwright's self-conscious interest in the artistic process, rather than in simple photographic realism and in the creation of an easy illusion. Tom, who is both player and observer, recreates the situations that led to his leaving by narrating and dramatizing a series of melodramatic family vignettes. The non-realistic technique of having Tom enter the action, or stand outside it as a commentator, is the 'illusion' to which Tom refers. However, it is more truthful than any realistic presentation might be, for Tom is indeed both in the action and outside it, living in the past as well as the present, both victim of his memories and master of them.

He returns to his past, to his mother's house, and dramatizes several episodes in his family's life centering on his sister and culminating in the disastrous visit of the 'gentleman caller'. Because he retains some ironic detachment from the scenes, the audience is at times distanced from Laura's fate. We see her through Tom's eyes, a kind of camera which brings the images closer at times and distances them at others. For instance, in Scene Six, the arrival of Jim, 'the most realistic character in the play' and 'an emissary from a world of reality' (23), is presented in the following manner:

> *The door swings shut, Laura is left alone. Legend on screen: 'Terror!' She utters a low moan and turns off the lamp – sits stiffly on the edge of the sofa, knotting her fingers together. Legend on screen: 'The Opening of a Door!' Tom and Jim appear on the fire escape steps and climb to the landing. Hearing their approach, Laura rises with a panicky gesture. She retreats to the portieres. The doorbell rings. Laura catches her breath and touches her throat. Low drums sound.* (74)

Tom's dramatizing memory has turned Laura into a melodramatic heroine of a silent movie with its sensationalizing announcements and its stylized acting. The play abounds in scenes of such decidedly cinematic, and specifically silent film, quality. Whereas in the silent movie the interspersing of text between the scenes served to intensify suspense and heighten emotion, here the effect is comical and the tone ironic.

However, it is not just from the past of Laura and Amanda that the screens distance the audience, but also from Tom who, as narrator, reveals something of himself through the use of this technique. 'Shakespeare', as he is called by his co-workers at the shoe factory, feels stifled by his job and by his mother and therefore tries to escape this claustrophobic atmosphere first by spending his evenings at the movies, then by leaving. It is then not surprising that when he returns to the past through memory, he should recall the scenes in cinematic terms. His family's histrionic temperaments and their attachment to the past naturally lend themselves to the sensibilities of the silent movie. By further over-dramatizing his hysterical mother and sister, Tom is able to separate himself emotionally.

By the time we meet Tom, he had left long ago, but never really left; now he returns in order to leave. Like Quentin, he remembers in order to forget, to be forgiven and to forgive himself. Referred to as the 'narrator', presented as 'an undisguised convention of the play' (22), Tom in fact fulfils several roles: he is stage manager, director, camera eye and confessional poet. He is all of these as well as a character in a melodrama of his own creation, a persona in Williams' play and the playwright's alter ego. Although he has generally been seen as an autobiographical figure, he is certainly not to be equated with Williams who maintains an ironic distance from Tom.[2] The kind of scenes Tom chooses to recall and the manner in which he has them reenacted, reveal as much about his character and his 'artistic' sensibilities, as they do about Amanda and Laura. The emotional signposts that Tom sets up punctuate the atmosphere of panic, urgency and hysteria that permeate Amanda's household, and indicate both Tom's ironic treatment of his mother and sister and his propensity for the most sentimental form of melodrama. While Tom may be satirizing his mother's and his sister's behavior through the use of melodrama, it is not entirely clear whether he is in fact able to distance himself from the form of expression to which he resorts. At times, one gets the distinct impression that 'Shakespeare' did not travel far in his artistic journey.

Tom is both part of the remembered action and outside it. He moves from the fire escape into the room within the action. The fire escape, *'a structure'*, William comments, *'whose name is a touch of accidental poetic truth, for all of these huge buildings are always burning with the slow and implacable fires of human desperation'* (21), is the means of entry into as well as escape from the past. It is also the entrance into and exit from reality; it is where Jim emerges. Unlike the Wingfield women, Tom's creations who reside in the past because they are fixed in Tom's memory, Tom is completely mobile, moving freely from past to present. Like other poet figures in Williams' plays, he is the 'fugitive kind', an outsider, a perpetual wanderer in space and in time. However, the nature of his wandering distinguishes him from Blanche or Val Xavier, for it constitutes not an aimless physical flight or a forced one, but a deliberate exploration. In the manner of the lyrical poet, Tom chooses to be an outsider to external reality and to reenter the past or the present at will. His total control of the developing action sets him apart from Williams' other 'fugitive kind' and enables him, in a manner similar to Quentin's, to overcome total self-absorption.

When he enters in Scene One to address the audience as the narrator of the play, he is dressed as a merchant seaman; during the course of the play we discover that Tom has joined the merchant marine to escape his suffocating *petit-bourgeois* existence. In particular, he flees from his mother who lives in a distant past of her own and from his sister and soul-mate Laura who, lacking Tom's artistic temperament and imagination, is tormented by her sense of being an outsider and forever imprisoned in her self-inflicted loneliness. As Thomas L. King points out in his essay 'Irony and Distance in *The Glass Menagerie*', 'Tom toys with the same madness in which his sister is trapped but saves himself with irony' (Parker 1983, 78). In other words, Tom's fate might have been like that of his sister – indeed Laura is a kind of alter-ego or soul-mate – had he not been able to understand and escape his environment.

Throughout the play, and particularly in Tom's soliloquies, there is a tension between nostalgia and irony. As King observes, each of Tom's speeches

> oscillates between a sentimental memory of the past, which draws the narrator into it, and a wry irony which keeps him from being fully engulfed and controlled by it . . . At times Tom seems almost deliberately to court disaster by creating for himself and the audience a memory so lovely and poignant that the pain of giving it up to return to reality is too much to bear, but return he does with mockery and a kind of wit that interrupts the witchery of memory just short of a withdrawn madness surrounded by soft music and a mind filled with 'delicate rainbow colors'. (78)

Possibly influenced by knowledge of the existence of mental illness in Williams' family and of Williams' own intimate relationship with his mentally ill sister Rose, King overstates the case somewhat when he speaks in terms of Tom toying with madness. Nonetheless, the tension to which King refers, as well as the tension between remembrance and forgetting, between loyalty and betrayal, is very much part of the emotional impact of this play, as it is of *Death of a Salesman, A Streetcar Named Desire* and *Long Day's Journey into Night*. Tom is torn between his need to forget and his need to remember. He cannot but be disloyal, for he is 'a poet with a job in a warehouse', a man who is 'not remorseless', but who must be pitiless in order 'to escape from the trap'. Still, he is haunted by his betrayal in the past and is in a sense forced to recreate over and over again the scenes that led to his decision. He not only controls the audience's reaction, but also monitors his own as he immerses himself in the memory.

Having 'a poet's weakness for symbols', he makes 'the gentleman caller' symbolize 'the long-delayed but always expected something that we live for' (23). Jim's visit constitutes the climax of the memory play because he represents Laura's first and last glimmer of hope of escape, a brief flirtation with reality and a promise of normalcy which ends in the shattering of illusions and in the loss of hope. Although Jim makes Laura believe for a moment that he might be her destined gentleman caller, he is in fact only displaying his natural charm when he asks her to dance with him. Quite apart from its sexual implications, the breaking of the glass unicorn's horn, during Laura and Jim's dance, on one hand reveals a 'normal' horse and on the other only a shattered and imperfect unicorn. Similarly, Laura seems to be more 'normal' and her physical deformity seems to disappear under the influence of Jim's native charm, but when Jim leaves the Wingfield household, he leaves behind a fragile creature unable to deal with reality.

It is this frailty and innocence of Laura that Tom is unable to forget. He is haunted by time, pursued by memories of the past which he is perpetually trying to escape. In Scene Five of the memory play Amanda reprimands Tom for ridiculing her 'plans and provisions':

> You are the only young man I know of who ignores the fact that the future becomes the present, the present the past, and the past turns into everlasting regret if you don't plan for it! (63)

Ironically enough, it is Tom who at this point lives in the future and Amanda who, in spite of her planning for Laura, lives in a past of her creation.

Tom describes his final leave-taking, his escape into the future, still believing that 'time is the longest distance between two places' (114). Unable to forget the past, the wanderer recalls his leaving:

> I traveled around a great deal. The cities swept about me like dead leaves, leaves that were brightly colored but torn away from branches. I would have stopped but I was pursued by something. I am walking along a street at night, in some strange city, before I have found companions. I pass the lighted window of a shop where perfume is sold. The window is filled with pieces of colored glass, tiny transparent bottles in delicate colors, like

> bits of shattered rainbow. Then all at once my sister touches my shoulder. I turn around and look into her eyes. Oh, Laura, Laura, I tried to leave you behind me, but I am more faithful than I intended to be! (115)

Tom is haunted by his betrayal of Laura, by his allowing her to become trapped in the past, and atones for his guilt through the faithful perpetual return, in his memory, to crucial scenes of that past. Through a cyclical process he is able, with the help of artistic recreation and aesthetic detachment, to free himself of the burden of the past, to exorcise his ghosts for a while till they return again.

Tom journeys back not only to Laura's world of suffused candle light and delicate glass animals and to Amanda's memories of genteel living, but also to America's adolescent awakening. Like Willy Loman, Blanche DuBois, Mary Tyrone and the people at Harry Hope's bar, he revisits an America of the past; in this play, as in a number of others, the return to a personal past is linked to a return to a public past. Visions of youthful innocence in these plays are accompanied by idealism concerning America's past. In this sense, the plays chronicle the public loss of innocence through a dramatization of a private fall from non-conscious existence. Characters such as Willy Loman, Blanche DuBois and Mary Tyrone repeatedly voice their faith in an ideal past – usually products of their imaginations – as they reject the future.

Looking at the past from the vantage point of a war-torn world, a 'world . . . lit by lightning' (115), Tom returns

> to that quaint period, the thirties, when the huge middle class of America was matriculating in a school for the blind. Their eyes had failed them, or they had failed their eyes, and so they were having their fingers pressed forcibly down on the fiery Braille alphabet of a dissolving economy. In Spain there was revolution. Here there was only shouting and confusion. In Spain there was Guernica. Here there were disturbances of labor, sometimes pretty violent. (23)

'This is the social background of the play', he explains. When he says good-bye to the memory of Laura and attempts to blow out her candles, he realizes that Laura's universe of the glass menagerie has no place in a fallen world. Unlike Amanda or Willy, he is able to take a critical attitude to the past and at the end of his recollection, he is able to extinguish the memory as he admonishes his sister: 'Blow out your candles, Laura – and so good bye . . . ' (115).

Within the past that Tom's memory recreates, Amanda and Laura live imprisoned in a past of their own, largely ignoring the social and economic realities not only in the world at large, but also in their immediate environment. Williams describes Amanda as

> *a little woman of great but confused vitality clinging frantically to another time and place . . . Certainly she has endurance and a kind of heroism, and though her foolishness makes her unwittingly cruel at times, there is tenderness in her slight person.* (stage directions, 5)

Like Blanche, she lives in the South of her youth when young men and women did not talk about 'anything coarse or common or vulgar', when among her gentlemen callers 'were some of the most prominent young planters of the Mississippi Delta – planters and sons of planters!' (26).

The economic realities of Amanda's present life bear little resemblance to the world of her memory. As the stage directions indicate:

> *The Wingfield apartment is in the rear of the building, one of those vast hive-like conglomerations of cellular living-units that flower as warty growths in overcrowded urban centers of lower middle-class population and are symptomatic of the impulse of this largest and fundamentally enslaved section of American society to avoid fluidity and differentiation and to exist and function as one interfused mass of automatism.* (21)

In the midst of this dehumanized environment, Amanda recounts her memories of the past and describes her dreams of the future. Laura is much 'too exquisitely fragile' (5) to survive life in such an environment without finding solace in her illusions. The tenement is

> *flanked on both sides by dark, narrow alleys which run into murky canyons of tangled clotheslines, garbage cans, and the sinister latticework of neighboring fire escapes.* (stage directions, 21)

This is where Amanda and Laura are fated to live out their lives because neither mother nor daughter has the freedom of Tom, primarily because she lacks his dynamic imagination and is restrained by both *petit-bourgeois* realities and ideas.

Because Tom has the gift of artistic creativity, he is able to establish some contact with reality and at the same time transcend that reality through art, a heroic feat of which Laura, physically and metaphorically crippled and braced, is not capable. Her clinging to a sheltered world of make-belief, her refuge in the childlike poetry of the tiny animals of the glass menagerie are her only defences against a world devoid of innocence. This form of escapism is also manifest in the figures of Brick Pollitt (in *Cat on a Hot Tin Roof*), the Tyrones (in *Long Day's Journey into Night*), Willy and Blanche, who escape from a fallen world into subjectivism and even madness in some cases. The only way out of this self-confinement is through the imagination and through artistic creation. The protagonists to whom these channels are not available – for instance Blanche and Willy – are mercilessly destroyed in the process of an equally intense self-scrutiny.

Characters such as Willy Loman or Blanche Dubois are suspended in a private region of their tormented conscience, unable to rejoin the 'sane' world of linear reality. The Loman house, stripped of clear physical boundaries, reflects the destructive mobility with which Willy moves from past to present to future. Similarly, Blanche is unable to control the intrusions of her past experiences into the present. In moments of mental confusion she involuntarily recalls the Varsouviana – the music that was playing when her husband killed himself. In *Death of a Salesman* and in *A Streetcar Named Desire* the expressionistic staging and the theme music are used to represent the characters' hallucinations and their immanent mental breakdown. By contrast, in *The Glass Menagerie* and in *After the Fall*, the anti-realistic elements are a function of the protagonists' artistic creation. In their yearning not only for innocence but also for timelessness and permanence, Quentin and Tom create an integral vision of their past and thus are able, at least temporarily it seems, to maintain their mental equilibrium. Their desire for a comprehensive vision of the world is fulfilled through their artistic and intellectual recreations.

In the process of their recreation of the past, Quentin and Tom are able to move beyond a paralyzing spiritual malaise into a state of acceptance. The self-consciousness – aesthetic in the case of the Williams play, intellectual in the Miller play – is so overwhelming that one can no longer speak of tragic form in these plays. Both Quentin and Tom exercise much greater control over their fates – that is, within the confines of the play – than is usually accorded tragic figures. Or, more precisely, even if they too are controlled by

'Fate' within the world of their plays, they are masters of that play and of their emotional and intellectual lives.

Indeed, it could be argued that *After the Fall* and *The Glass Menagerie* take as their starting point what one would expect to be the culminating point of most tragedies, that is what Gassner calls 'tragic enlightenment' and Anderson refers to as 'recognition', or the protagonist's belated awareness. From the outset of *The Glass Menagerie* and of *After the Fall,* Tom and Quentin are in a state of fully articulated awareness which leads them into further self-exploration. Unlike Willy, Blanche, Val Xavier, John Proctor and countless other characters, they need no longer struggle with the outside world. Their fully internalized and isolated battles preclude the tragic clash with external forces, and the internalized conflict is temporarily resolved through an aesthetic and intellectual transcendence of self-consciousness. *After the Fall* and *The Glass Menagerie* may dramatize tragic situations – Laura and Amanda Wingfield's fate and the fates of the people Quentin's memory recalls may be tragic – but they are not tragedies.

Lionel Abel's distinction, in his influential *Metatheatre* (1963), between Greek tragedy and post-Renaissance self-conscious theatre is useful here. Abel argues that except for Ibsen's social plays and nineteenth and twentieth-century realism and naturalism, all western drama from Shakespeare on, and including some of his own plays, is metatheatre because it is peopled by self-dramatizing, highly self-conscious protagonists. Because the metaplay shows a world which is a projection of human consciousness and is therefore theatre about theatre, it is anti-tragic. Abel maintains that the increasing self-awareness and self-consciousness of the hero have made genuine tragedy untenable. Thus he equates the term tragedy with Greek tragedy which he employs as the fundamental form to which subsequent forms make reference. While the relegation of all non-classical tragedy to the category of metatheatre is contingent on a very rigid definition of tragedy, Abel's discussion of dramatic self-consciousness and of the self-dramatizing propensities of western protagonists is valuable because it places modern subjectivism into a historical perspective.

Self-dramatization can of course have a whole range of manifestations, from Blanche's histrionic outbursts to Tom's and Quentin's careful orchestrations of memory plays. Whether in *Hamlet* – where, according to Abel one encounters the quintessential self-dramatized hero – or in the modern plays under discussion, the self-dramatizing hero's necessary self-reflection provides the heroic intensity. In *Death of a Salesman* it is a tragic flaw of sorts because it destroys the protagonist; it is a mark of non-tragic heroism in *The Glass Menagerie* and in *After the Fall* where it functions as a liberating device. While the intensity inherent in self-reflection provides a version of heroism in such diverse plays as *Death of a Salesman, After the Fall* and *The Glass Menagerie,* it is also indicative of the increasing subjectivism of a current of modern drama in the decades following the Second World War and of a potentially destructive self-absorption on the part of the protagonist. Furthermore, it points to a withdrawal from an external world, perceived as hostile, into a world not only of imagination but also of tormented conscience. Invariably, in the plays under discussion, self-reflection is inseparable from self-trial, self-condemnation and the desire for forgiveness.

Tragedy requires a balance of self-consiousness and unawareness, or of unawareness followed by belated awareness. As a result of the lack of such a balance, tragedy is circumvented in *After the Fall* and in *The Glass Menagerie* where the protagonists transcend despair and gain control of their fate through the transfiguring power of the imaginative process. Tom's self-conscious dramatization and Quentin's articulated intellectualization preclude the development from lack of vision to belated awareness associated with tragic heroes.

By contrast, in *Death of a Salesman* and in *A Streetcar Named Desire* the protagonists are tragically destroyed as a result of their alienating internalization of conflicts and their inability to deal with the outside world which imposes its own laws upon them. Their quests end in only partial and imperfect enlightenment. Here destructive self-consciousness prevails, and creative, deliberate self-dramatization cannot take place.

5
Survival as Heroism

Key Largo, A Streetcar Named Desire and *Death of a Salesman* posit heroism in the idealist's unsuccessful struggle in an essentially materialistic society, a struggle that is seen as conferring dignity on the protagonist. Through their opposition to the system and to social mores, and through their resulting demise, the protagonists validate their otherwise meaningless existence. They find themselves in the valueless world described by such critics as Krutch and Fergusson. It is what might be called a post-heroic world in that it no longer understands heroism or has any need for it. These plays delineate an indifferent or hostile environment from which the hero or heroine nonetheless emerges the triumphant moral victor, if not an actual one, by virtue of his or her estrangement and exile from the materialistic and philistine external world.

O'Neill's conception, in his early career, of the striving individual's tragic fate, is characteristic of this approach to heroism. He believes that:

> A man wills his own defeat when he pursues the unattainable. But his *struggle* is his success! He is an example of the spiritual significance which life attains when it aims high enough, when the individual fights all the hostile forces within and without himself to achieve a future of nobler values. (Törnqvist, *A Drama of Souls,* 14)

Therefore, tragedy resides in the surpassing of one's own limits and in the doomed struggle for the unattainable. O'Neill places special emphasis on what might ordinarily be construed as failure. The person who engages in these failed battles, O'Neill believes, is 'necessarily tragic'. However, he 'is not depressing; he is exhilarating! He may be a failure in our materialistic sense. His treasures are in other kingdoms. Yet isn't he the most inspiring of all successes?' (Törnqvist, *A Drama of Souls*, 14) As a consequence, this type of protagonist may be deemed morally and spiritually superior to others and to the environment because of heightened awareness and special sensibility. His or her 'success' resides in the willingness to undertake the idealistic struggle. Indeed, the greater the failure, the greater the success, it seems.

In the martyr plays, the heroic individuals are forced by circumstances to directly confront the hostile society as their idealism is put to the test. In a sense, plays such as *Joan of Lorraine, The Crucible* and *Journey to Jerusalem* offer a further intensification of the heroic idealism which figures in *Key Largo* and in *Elizabeth the Queen.* Both types of play affirm the value of idealism, as they attest to the heroism of an act of faith. The difference is of degree, not of kind. And even more importantly, they equate heroism with the willingness to undergo intense suffering, physical in terms of traditional martyr plays, mental and emotional in the modern variations on the martyr play. This equation of heroism with suffering is made not only by O'Neill but also by Miller and Williams, especially by the latter. For instance, as we have seen, Williams maintains that Blanche's stature, her 'size' as a personality, has to do with her intensity of feeling (*Memoirs*, 235). Similarly, it may be argued that Willy Loman's stature is not a function of a democratically minded audience that would grant importance to a 'common man' but rather one of Willy's own intensity and consuming self-absorption. In *Long Day's Journey into Night*, the alienation, which is both the cause and the result of self-consciousness and internalization, is seen as the only viable alternative to a tortured existence and as the only means of escape from undesirable reality.

The diverse reinterpretations of heroism found in *Death of a Salesman, Key Largo, Joan of Lorraine, Orpheus Descending, A Streetcar Named Desire* and *The Crucible*, to name just a few, fill a need for faith and for an affirmation of human dignity in an age perceived by some writers as spiritually impoverished and morally diminished. While dramatizing the idealists' aloneness and alienation, the plays restate the hero's or heroine's capacity for suffering and their willingness to undergo anguish. In contrast to these plays, O'Neill's *The Iceman Cometh* (1939/46)[1] and *Long Day's Journey into Night* (1941/56)[2] and Williams' *Cat on a Hot Tin Roof* (1955)[3] challenge the very possibility of meaningful action (whether external or internalized) and of heroism, as they dramatize a series of deadlocked conflicts. No longer is tragedy a function of a specific individual personality or of a particular fate; rather, existence itself is deemed tragic. However, this approach should not be confused with Sartre's theatre of situation ('Forgers of Myths'), or with its classical antecedent, the Aristotelian concept of the primacy of plot. These plays still focus on individual psychology, and motivation is primarily psychological; however, specific individuals are not singled out or treated exclusively. Rather, the tragic view of life is dramatized.

Because they show the tragedy of existence, all three plays rely on the dramatization of group interaction. Where plays such as *Orpheus Descending, All My Sons, Death of a Salesman, A Streetcar Named Desire* and *The Crucible* dramatize the individual's confrontation with other individuals and his or her survival in society, *Cat on a Hot Tin Roof, The Iceman Cometh* and *Long Day's Journey into Night* are primarily concerned with individuals in terms of the group. This is not to say that specific characters are not individualized or that their fate is totally subordinated to the fate of the collective. However, in all three plays, and especially in the carefully orchestrated *Long Day's Journey into Night*, the individual members of the group, even when pitted against each other, are dramatized in terms of the group whose cohesiveness is continually being tested. For instance, *Cat on a Hot Tin Roof* is not so much about Brick's moral paralysis, Maggie's sexual frustration or Big Daddy's cancer as it is about a more general state of spiritlessness, dramatized through relationships within the Pollitt family.

In the stage directions Williams insists on a wider, not solely personal, interpretation of Brick's situation:

> *The bird that I hope to catch in the net of this play is not the solution of one man's psychological problem. I'm trying to catch the true quality of experience in a group of people, that cloudy, flickering, evanescent – fiercely charged! – interplay of live human beings in the thundercloud of a common crisis.* (85)

This 'common crisis' refers, on the one hand, to the condition of 'mendacity', the loss of value exemplified in varying degrees by Big Daddy, Gooper and Maggie, and on the other hand, to the 'truth', the clinging to purity exemplified by Brick. In the most reductionist manner, the former has to do with an aggressive survival of the fittest, the latter with a detachment from life or a death-wish. And it is these two diametrically opposed approaches to life that form the central conflict in this play and to a lesser extent in the two O'Neill plays. Both responses to life are accompanied by suffering because both involve the protagonist in an intense struggle with others and with the self.

Miller comments at length on *Cat on a Hot Tin Roof* in his essay 'The Shadows of the Gods' and praises Williams' 'very evident determination to unveil and engage the widest range of causation conceivable to him' (189). He believes that it is Williams' challenge to society's right to survival that gives this play tragic significance and maintains that:

> The question here . . . the ultimate question is the right of society to renew itself when it is, in fact, unworthy. There is, after all, a highly articulated struggle for material power going on here. There is literally and symbolically a world to forsake and damn . . . There is a moral judgment hanging over this play which never quite comes down. (191)

Characteristically, he phrases in terms of social conflict what is essentially an existential question. Therefore he assesses the significance of the playwright's challenge in social terms:

> The question of society's right to insist upon its renewal when it is unworthy is a question of tragic grandeur, and those who have asked this question of the world know full well the lash of its retaliation. ('The Shadows of the Gods', 192)

Perhaps because he views the problem in this manner, he is perturbed by the fact that the conflict between Brick's viewpoint and that of his father is left unresolved at the end of the play. He insists that:

> Above the father's and the son's individual viewpoints the third must emerge, the viewpoint, in fact, of the audience, the society, and the race. It is a viewpoint that must weigh . . . the question of its own right to biological survival – and one thing more, the question of the fate of the sensitive and the just in an impure world of power. (192)

However, Williams is not interested in a clear resolution or in taking sides. His main purpose is not only to ask 'the question of the fate of the sensitive and just in an impure world of power', but also to indicate the precariousness of a situation in which one alternative is a deadlocked sterility and the other is a corrupt virility. Thus any possibility of a future is associated with corruption and decay, just as life is ultimately associated with degeneration and death. In this sense, Brick's refusal to partake in Big Daddy's version of life and to procreate also marks a desire for permanence. If Big Daddy represents temporal change and nature in all its vitality and vulgarity, Brick stands for the desire for immortality and the resistance to change.

Therefore, the choice, as dramatized in the play, is actually not between two opposing worlds or two competing societies but rather between renewal and extinction. The play may be seen as a satire on humanity's acquisitive drive and as a homosexual playwright's farcical treatment not only of bourgeois marriage and family but also of the procreative impulse. Greed in the play is viewed in terms of fundamental 'human nature' and of basic survival. One could even say that the Pollitts (whose name echoes 'politic', 'pollute', 'polled' and 'pollinate') represent a patriarchial Everyfamily and that the conflict between Big Daddy and Brick is the stereotypical conflict of generations, exacerbated by the fact that Brick (and perhaps even Big Daddy?) may or may not be a homosexual.

The ideas of human survival and of a moribund civilization struggling to renew itself are central to *Cat on a Hot Tin Roof* and often obscured by critical discussions of Brick's fate as an isolated phenomenon. Criticism of this type usually centres solely on the sexual aspects of the themes of betrayal and mendacity. For example, in 'The Desperate Morality of the Plays of Tennessee Williams', Arthur Ganz focuses on a discussion of sexual rejection which, he asserts, constitutes the main conflict in a number of Williams' plays. In an even narrower vein, John Orr argues in *Tragic Drama and Modern Society* that the play is serious but not tragic because its homosexual theme is too specific to admit a wider significance. However, it is not homosexuality that is the issue here but rather, as in *A Streetcar Named Desire,* betrayal. Furthermore, it is not just Brick's betrayal of Skipper or Big Daddy's self-betrayal that is significant, but a betrayal which is systemic and forms a recurring pattern. In terms of dramatic tragedy it constitutes the transgression for which suffering is the punishment. Big Daddy's greed and materialism, like Willy Loman's self-delusion and dedication to false values, have a high price. Similarly, Brick must bear the consequences of his decision to remain an outsider and thus must betray life.

The father's betrayal of the son – in *Death of a Salesman* and in *Cat on a Hot Tin Roof* – leads to his rejection by the son or, to put it into terms which carry wider interpretation, to the rejection of the past by the present and to a futureless reality. The spiritual wasteland offered by Big Daddy, in the form of total self-sacrifice to material values, is the inheritance Brick refuses to accept because he is unwilling to perpetuate the transgressions of past generations and, it seems, unable to procreate and thus to create a new generation.[4] As a result, he opts for a different but similarly demoralizing fate: death-in-life. Biff's self-defeating attitude to life is a comparable response – albeit on a smaller scale for it lacks the wider implications of Brick's protest – to his father's betrayal of values. On a larger, social, non-familial scale, the capitulation of the denizens of Harry Hope's bar and their withdrawal from the outside world are also functions of profound disillusionment and betrayal of genuine idealism.

The struggle for survival, Bid Daddy reassures Brick, is an ignoble business ending in degeneration, decay and death, but it must be pursued because the only other alternative is death-in-life. This dilemma between life and death – between mendacity and truth – is presented in terms which lend themselves to schematization, but in fact such reductionism does not account for their complexity. Not only is the truth 'rarely pure and never simple', as Oscar Wilde observed, neither is mendacity. Daddy's grandeur – his sheer energy and daring – lies in his adamant clinging to life in spite of his recognition of the pervasiveness of mendacity. As Maggie, herself a survivor, says 'life has got to be allowed to continue even after the *dream* of life is – all – over' (44). Conversely, Brick's heroism – if it may be called that – lies in his insistence on the truth. Williams refers to him as *'a broken, "tragically elegant" figure telling simply as much as he knows of "the Truth"'* (90). Unwilling to participate in procreation and in the further proliferation of Pollitts, Brick is an outsider, an aloof observer of the struggle for survival and the competition for material goods, and a defeated commentator on truth and beauty.

O'Neill is less directly interested than Williams in dramatizing this type of competitive struggle for survival. Rather, in *The Iceman Cometh* and in *Long Day's Journey into Night*, he shows characters who are beyond the stage of aggressive survival. Unlike the Pollitts, who are motivated by avarice and lust and who are best described in animal terms, the Tyrones are, like Brick, 'almost not alive', ghosts drifting through an unreal landscape trying to escape reality through alcohol and drugs. At best, they tolerate life rather than live it; they endure rather than survive.

According to O'Neill, fate no longer has the same meaning as in classical tragedy; however, life itself constitutes inexorable fate. As he puts it:

> In Greek tragedy the characters are inexorably pushed on the road by fate . . . Life itself is the same as that. You get on the road and no matter what you do or how you try to change or correct your life, you can't do it, because Fate, or Kismet, or whatever you call it, will push you down the road. (Gelb and Gelb, 352)

Mary Tyrone, in *Long Day's Journey into Night*, echoes this fatalistic philosophy of life when she remarks that since we have no control over what life does to us, what it makes of us, all we can hope for is acceptance and forgiveness. The dark pessimism of the play and the characters' stoical acceptance of determinism is best embodied in her important lines:

> None of us can help the things life has done to us. They're done before you realize it, and once they're done they make you do other things until at last everything comes between you and what you'd like to be, and you've lost your true self forever. (61)

This fundamental determinism is destructive to individual integrity and seems to preclude the possibility of free will. Furthermore, according to this ideology, one can never escape the past which, Mary tells us, 'is the present . . . It's the future, too. We all try to lie out of that but life won't let us' (87). As a consequence, one also has no control over the future. The belief in the determinism of the past and in its victimization of individuals, to the point of moral and spiritual paralysis, is the guiding concept in the two O'Neill plays and to some extent in *Cat on a Hot Tin Roof*. In the Williams play, however, there is still an operative free will and characters seem to have control over their actions. In the two O'Neill plays, and particularly in *Long Day's Journey into Night*, one finds a mixture of fatalism and guilt.

In order to keep despair and disillusion at bay, the characters in *The Iceman Cometh*, *Long Day's Journey into Night* and *Cat on a Hot Tin Roof* earnestly cultivate philosophical detachment and self-delusion. They retreat mentally into memory and imagination, moving either into a world of illusion and hope or into one of total carefree oblivion. They attempt to escape the falseness of existence by creating new sets of falsities. In *The Iceman Cometh* the shattering of one pipe dream is usually followed by the creation of a new one, as every new perception of reality proves to be an illusion. The characters' various perceptions and transformations of their meaningless lives and their combat against skepticism constitute the action and provide the heroic intensity.

And yet, in the O'Neill play, as in his *Long Day's Journey into Night* and in *Cat on a Hot Tin Roof*, the crisis of faith seems total and irreversible, the lack of genuine idealism a given, the existential unease overwhelming. So much so, that the kind of argument Anderson puts forth in *Key Largo* in defense of idealistic action – that is, that it is precisely the cynical and materialistic nature of the world that requires an idealistic personal outlook, that it is the pervasive faithlessness that engenders faith – would be not only impossible but futile in the shattered world of these plays. Those characters who still harbor some semblance of idealism – such as Brick Pollitt and Mary Tyrone – live in a subjective world of fantasy and are totally paralyzed by their refusal to accept the reality of the outside world. Brick partakes of both nihilism and the occasional idealism when he recalls the purity of his relationship with Skipper.

Thus idealism here exists only in the debased form of self-delusion or of cynical detachment; faith exists only as the desperate clinging to meaning. As a result, the characters in these plays vacillate between a proud appropriation of the spiritual void (Brick's, Edmund Tyrone's and Larry Slade's responses) and a blind refusal to submit to an overwhelming sense of futility (Maggie Pollitt's, Mary Tyrone's and the Harry Hope bar residents' responses). Locked in their solipsistic universes, they are forced to coexist and – to paraphrase Maggie's remark to Brick in *Cat on a Hot Tin Roof* – they do not live together, only occupy the same cage. The self-enclosed space of each person's consciousness and the circumscribed common space of the action (the Tyrones' living room, Harry Hope's bar, Brick and Maggie's bed-sitting-room) function as both safe havens from the hostilities and uncertainties of the outside world and as prisons where the individuals are fated to torment each other for the duration of their lives.

Interestingly enough, *Long Day's Journey into Night* and *The Iceman Cometh* are set at the time of an important turning point in O'Neill's life – summer 1912. In that year he attempted suicide, was diagnosed as having tuberculosis and later decided to become a playwright (Törnqvist, *A Drama of Souls*, 17). These plays of the lower depths take place during the year that the playwright virtually returned from the dead and was not only reconciled to living but chose to dedicate himself to his new-found profession. In the autobiographical *Long Day's Journey into Night*, the specific family crisis may be seen in wider terms. Although the drama is one family's ritual of reconciliation and one playwright's attempt to put to rest the ghosts of his past, its preoccupation with existential unease, with the conflicting desires to 'belong' and to remain in a subjective universe, take it beyond the autobiographical genre.

In *Long Day's Journey into Night* life is seen as a stumbling through fog – characterized by pain, loss and yearning – with only the occasional clarity of vision. Indeed, the fog is desirable for it softens the harsh outlines of reality. Only through forgetfulness is existence made bearable and only through forgiveness is coexistence made tolerable. What replaces idealism and faith in *Long Day's Journey into Night* are the characters' knowledge of a mutual fate and their frustrated but nonetheless deep-seated love for each other which often takes the form of bitter recrimination. Ironically enough, it is their reluctant resignation to fate that strengthens their determination to endure. James Tyrone and his sons can do little by understanding Mary's morphine addiction and Mary herself urges James to forego trying to understand:

> James! We've loved each other! We always will! Let's remember only that, and not try to understand what we cannot understand, or help things that cannot be helped – the things life has done to us we cannot excuse or explain. (85)

For O'Neill, for whom the need for forgiveness was the motivation in the writing of this play, the cultivation of illusions and a desperate refuge in a common fate are the only means of escape from despair left to a morally and spiritually shattered humanity.

Unlike *The Glass Menagerie*, also an autobiography, this play has no mediating persona, no one to prevent the audience from being completely drawn into the action of this play *'of old sorrow, written in tears and blood'*. It was written, O'Neill confesses in the 1941 dedication to Carlotta Monterey, *'with deep pity and understanding and forgiveness for* all *the four haunted Tyrones'*. These tortured souls of the play are trapped not by their past choices, but by what the past had presumably done to them; they are being emotionally and physically destroyed in the process of living. An overpowering sense of fate hangs over the Tyrone household as the family members journey into the oblivion of night, and by implication death.

Mary is tormented by the awareness that she never had a real home, that her itinerant actor husband was unable to provide her with one, partly because of the demands of his career, partly as a result of his tight-fistedness. Her husband, in turn, is discomfited by his past choices, angered and saddened that he chose financial security as a matinee idol over a less lucrative career as a Shakespearean actor. It soon becomes apparent in the course of the play that Mary's sense of rootlessness and alienation goes beyond the continually voiced familial maladjustment. Her morphine-induced journeys into the past, into delusion and into oblivion constitute an attempt to escape present reality, to authenticate the self and to find something to which she can belong – a frequent quest of a number of O'Neill's protagonists, particularly in his early plays. In Mary's case, belonging means a sense of being part of a family and implies the comfort of Catholicism. Although she repeatedly voices her desire for a stable family life, she in fact continues to escape into the past, into her innocent convent youth when she wanted to be a nun or a concert pianist. She hopes to rediscover the faith and optimism she believes she had had before she met James Tyrone and her life was changed forever.

Her attempt to regain faith by journeying into the past is akin to Blanche DuBois' clinging to illusions of nobility and innocence, to Brick Pollitt's crippling refusal to relinquish a memory of a true friendship or to Val Xavier's ideal of purity and incorruptibility. This memory of an uncorrupted past, even if inexact because recreated by desire, provides the only comfort in an imperfect world and the only sense of a genuine identity. The awareness of the loss of a former, innocent self is a source of anguish for such characters as Blanche DuBois, Willy Loman, Mary Tyrone and Brick Pollitt. In wider terms, America's loss of innocence can be seen as a source of anguish for the playwright.

As a result of having lost faith and of having become a victim of the past, Mary has lost her true identity. She senses the falseness of her existence:

> I've become such a liar. I never lied about anything once upon a time. Now I have to lie, especially to myself . . . I've never

> understood anything about it, except that one day long ago I found I could no longer call my soul my own. (93)

According to the characters' perception, here and in *Cat on a Hot Tin Roof*, loss of hope and faith has to do with a falsification of the self. Ironically enough, the return to what is perceived by these characters as an innocent state is linked to a complete loss of the self to an intoxicated obliteration of the present. Thus the choice seems to be between the disingenuousness of present reality and the falsehood of a remembered past. Relying on morphine to give her comfort and to take her back into her past, Mary lives in the hope of regaining her faith one day and returning 'home'.

Her profound estrangement is further articulated by Edmund, the younger son and the O'Neill figure. O'Neill gives the name Eugene to the dead son of the Tyrones and the name Edmund – the name of his younger brother who died in infancy – to Jamie's tubercular younger brother. Mary's desire to return to her 'home' of the past is nothing short of a death wish, a need which is comparable to Edmund's desire to be an organic part of the nature, specifically the sea. In Act Four, Edmund describes to his father his existential dread and his yearning for non-material existence and for the oblivion of death:

> It was a mistake, my being born a man, I would have been much more successful as a sea gull or a fish. As it is, I will always be a stranger who never feels at home, who does not really want and is not really wanted, who can never belong, who must always be a little in love with death! (153–4)

As the night progresses, Edmund speaks of his powerful yearning to be part of the protective fog which gradually engulfs the house and provides a haven for all the Tyrones:

> The fog was where I wanted to be . . . Everything looked and sounded unreal. Nothing was what it is. That's what I wanted – to be alone with myself in another world where truth is untrue and life can hide from itself. (131)

The Tyrones alternate between drifting apart and being brought together by their shared alienation. While struggling to maintain their emotional and mental balance, the mother and the two sons voice their death-wishes.

Indeed, Edmund's mystical experience by the sea seems to be a premonition of death:

> . . . I even lost the feeling of being on land. The fog and the sea seemed part of each other. It was like walking on the bottom of the sea. As if I had drowned long ago. As if I was a ghost belonging to the fog, and the fog was the ghost of the sea. I felt damned peaceful to be nothing more than a ghost within a ghost. (131)

Like Mary, as well as the main characters in plays such as *Cat on a Hot Tin Roof*, *Death of a Salesman*, *A Streetcar Named Desire* and *The Iceman Cometh*, Edmund finds peace in escaping reality and, like these other characters, knows that to face reality means to die in spirit: 'Who wants to see life as it is, if they can help it? It's the three Gorgons in one. You look in their faces and turn to stone. Or it's Pan. You see him and you die – that is, inside you – and have to go on living as a ghost' (131). Life on the edge of reality seems to describe the very nature of existence in this play; the escape from reality signifies a search for an alternative, non-material existence, a search which is associated with both mystical experience and a death-wish.

In this connection, Törnqvist, in his *A Drama of Souls*, comments on O'Neill's ideas concerning human fate, specifically his mysticism. Törnqvist asserts that O'Neill's reference to Strindberg's drama as 'behind-life'

> relates directly to O'Neill's concept of fate. It suggests the existence of an external, supernatural force ruling man's life, what Strindberg termed 'the Powers' and O'Neill simply called 'Fate' or 'God'. It also indicates the existence of an internal, psychological fate. In Strindberg's chamber plays the veil of the material world is often momentarily torn apart and beyond its floating shreds we divine both a supernatural world, a product of Strindberg's religious concern, and a subterranean one, a creation of the author's keen psychological insight. (34)

Edmund yearns for a vision of this other world where he would be at one with nature but is denied all but the occasional glimpse of it. He confesses 'with alcoholic talkativeness' to having lived in a perpetual fog with only a few isolated moments of vision:

> And several other times in my life, when I was swimming far out, or lying alone on the beach, I have had the same experience. Became the sun, the hot sand, green seaweed anchored to a rock, swaying in the tide. Like a saint's vision of beatitude. Like the veil of things as they seem drawn back by an unseen hand. For a second you see – and seeing the secret, are the secret. For a second there is meaning! Then the hand lets the veil fall and you are alone, lost in the fog again, and you stumble on toward nowhere, for no good reason! (153)

He describes to his father these rare moments of belonging as he tells of his experiences at sea. On one such occasion, he says:

> I became drunk with the beauty and the singing rhythm of it, and for a moment I lost myself – actually lost my life. I was set free! I dissolved in the sea, became white sails and flying spray, became beauty and rhythm, became moonlight and the ship and the high dim-starred sky! I belonged, without past or future, within peace and unity and a wild joy, within something greater than my own life, or the life of Man, to Life itself! (153)

Another time he experienced 'the moment of ecstatic freedom . . . the joy of belonging to a fulfilment beyond men's lousy, pitiful, greedy fears and hopes and dreams!'

The fog gradually envelops the stage and reinforces the sense of the unreality of existence, the idea of life as a waking nightmare where the living dead enact their fears and desires. At the same time, this semi-conscious existence is shown to be preferable to the pain of total awareness. By Act Three '*Dusk is gathering in the living room, an early dusk due to the fog which has rolled in from the Sound and is like a white curtain drawn down outside the windows*'. The foghorn sounds '*like a mournful whale in labor*' (97) and seems to wail like a banshee as it heralds oblivion and death.

Mary, who is described as a ghost (137), also loves the fog because it provides a barrier between her and the inimical world of reality which threatens to rob her of the hope of returning home. In spite of all her attempts to regain her girlish quality, however, she is by this point in the play '*an aging, cynically sad, embittered woman*' (107); James Tyrone, who observes her increasing estrangement from reality, is described as '*a sad, bewildered, broken old man*' (123). At the end of the act, James Tyrone predicts that Mary will be a 'mad ghost before the night's over' (123), but Mary is already too far removed to understand.

The Tyrones' journey into the night is a journey of mutual accusations and recriminations culminating, in Act Four, in a series of intoxicated confessions. It is a journey through alcohol and morphine, into the fog of forgetfulness and into partial forgiveness. Louis Sheaffer observes in his biography of O'Neill that

> as the family members seek at once exoneration and forgiveness – they are forever admitting and denying their offenses in almost the same breath – the play develops, in piecemeal fashion, into a series of confessions. For all his early apostasy, the author could not root out the effect of his Catholic upbringing; the Tyrones' living room gradually takes on the character of a confessional. (*O'Neill. Son and Artist*, 513–14)

Indeed, the whole play may be seen as a confession of sorts for O'Neill. The playwright described *Long Day's Journey into Night* to George Jean Nathan as

> a deeply tragic play, but without any violent dramatic action. At the final curtain, there they still are, trapped within each other by the past, each guilty and at the same time innocent, scorning, loving, pitying each other, understanding and yet not understanding at all, forgiving but still doomed never to be able to forget. (*O'Neill. Son and Artist*, 509)

According to O'Neill, it is the fact that characters are fated to replay the same scenes, to engage in the same conflicts over and over again, that constitutes the tragedy.

By the beginning of the confessional fourth act, it is midnight, and '*the wall of fog appears denser than ever*' (125). Tyrone, drunk but very much self-aware, is '*a sad, defeated old man, possessed by hopeless resignation*' (125). The only hope for these somnabulistic fog people is total detachment from reality and truth through a journey into the past and into illusion. Mary is well on her way to this region far removed from the present. Under the influence of morphine she gradually takes refuge in the memories of her youth. Already in Act Three

> *Mary is paler than before and her eyes shine with unnatural brilliance. The strange detachment in her manner has intensified. She has hidden*

> *deeper within herself and found refuge and release in a dream where present reality is but an appearance to be accepted and dismissed unfeelingly – even with a hard cynicism – or entirely ignored.* (97)

By the end of the play, as the curtain falls, she has accomplished her return journey and appears on the stage carrying her wedding gown.

Unlike Mary and Edmund, who seek respite from the pain of reality, the elder son Jamie appropriates the darkest vision of humanity. In order to render his condition tolerable, Jamie, like Larry Slade in *The Iceman Cometh*, adopts a cynical Mephistophelian stance. To his father's great consternation, Jamie deliberately immerses himself in the poetry of Baudelaire, Swinburne and Dowson, in the philosophy of Nietzsche and Schopenhauer, and in the drama of Strindberg. But unlike Larry's disillusionment with humanity, a result of his youthful dedication to political ideals, Jamie's pessimism, like that of so many characters in modern American drama, seems to be constitutional.

Whereas through Edmund O'Neill dramatizes his propensity for mysticism as well as his desire for communion and through Mary his yearning for escape, through the character of Jamie he voices his nihilism. Together the mother and the two sons represent the various forms of resistance to the patriarchial figure of James Tyrone who, it emerges in the course of the play, is partly responsible for their 'fates'. It was James' injudicious economizing that led to Mary's morphine addiction and that now endangers Edmund's frail physical condition. And it is also this related concern for financial security that has been responsible for Tyrone's ruined career. Although Mary's morphine-induced journey seems to be the central concern throughout the play and to bring the three men together, it is Tyrone's past decisions and actions that are the focus of the family's discussions. Tyrone is held responsible for their lives; in fact, he seems to be on trial for having determined his family's fate.

Although he, too, drinks himself into forgetfulness, he remains in contact with reality perhaps the longest. He may not revert to the past in the manner of his wife, but he is clearly the voice of an untenable past and of a Christian humanism that has no place in the new century. Jamie and Edmund, on the other hand, stand on the threshold of the twentieth century and represent the new era of hopelessness. The conflict between James Tyrone and his sons is partly a conflict between a disturbing vision of a new era and an unreliable memory of a lost one.

In this play, as well as in *The Iceman Cometh*, the first two decades of the century are presented as ones of disillusionment and profound cynicism, possibly more so when viewed from the vantage point of the forties and fifties. The denizens of Harry Hope's bar and the elder Tyrones look to the nineteenth century for solace. In *Long Day's Journey into Night*, O'Neill explores the modern malaise in terms of his own family; in *The Iceman Cometh* he views this same disillusionment with modern life and with existence itself in terms of a larger group of individuals brought together by a shared fate. In the latter play, most idealistic causes and human achievements are shown to be fraudulent, and there is little optimism regarding heroic action. The characters we meet in Harry Hope's bar have all given up an active existence after having engaged in various key events at the turn of the century. In particular, the bar is peopled by former members of the anarchist-syndicalist movement who have since relinquished any political idealism and have only their 'pipe-dreams' on which to depend.

Their pessimism and inertia reflect O'Neill's own disillusionment in the forties. As Louis Sheaffer indicates in *O'Neill: Son and Artist*, O'Neill's

> view of the human condition and mankind's prospects had long been darkening; he had abandoned virtually all hope of Progress, Civilization, the Future, a perspective that the war in Europe seemed to confirm. Life appeared to him by now, as his new drama suggests, essentially a fraud. (489)

This skepticism regarding social causes as well as private lives also characterizes the attitude of Larry Slade, a former syndicalist-anarchist whom the playwright has comment: 'The material the ideal free society must be constructed from is men themselves and you can't build a marble temple out of a mixture of mud and manure' (30). Between the wars O'Neill seemed to have lost faith not only in 'human nature' but also in all organized socio-political causes and, as the following statement shows, was amused by other people's faith:

> Time was when I was an active socialist, and after that, a philosophical anarchist. But today I can't feel that anything

like that really matters. It is rather amusing to me to see how seriously people take politics and social questions and how much they expect of them. Life as a whole is changed very little, if at all, as a result of their course. (Gelb and Gelb, 387)

By the time he wrote *The Iceman Cometh* O'Neill had abandoned all hope in human progress and had little faith in social ameliorism. Larry's statement, however, is more profoundly pessimistic than a dismissal of the importance of socio-political issues. Like Jamie's and Edmund Tyrone's remarks, it exudes a loss of faith in humanity and ultimately in life. O'Neill had engaged in what Travis Bogard calls a 'long poetically oriented quest'. Following this quest

conducted through the plays of the 1920's, seeking a God to which men could belong . . . [O'Neill] at last has come to agree with Nietzsche that men live in a Godless world. There is no longer the possibility of being possessed by Dionysian ecstasy. Men's dreams can have no fulfillment that is not in itself illusion; the mindless, unpoetic materialism of each of the dreams is sufficient testimony to the fact that in all the outer world there is nowhere to go, nothing worth having, nothing to which man may make offering as to a God. (*Contour in Time,* 415)

Larry echoes O'Neill's nihilism of the period; he has come to the conclusion that people do not want to be saved, 'for that would mean they'd have to give up greed, and they'll never pay that price for liberty' (11). This knowledge has led him to forsake the Movement. However, he left also because he discovered that he was 'born condemned to be one of those who has to see all sides of a question' (30). As a result, he could never find easy solutions and saw only complicated questions. Again, it is a combination of personal and political factors that has led to great disillusionment.

Like Edmund, he repeatedly voices his death wish. Living out the rest of his life in Harry Hope's bar, he prides himself on having taken 'a seat in the grandstand of philosophical detachment' (11), on being able to observe human folly from a distance and espouses an aware, decadent life-weariness:

All I know is I'm sick of life! I'm through! I've forgotten myself! I'm drowned and contented on the bottom of a bottle. Honor or dishonor, faith or treachery are nothing to me but the opposites

> of the same stupidity which is ruler and king of life, and in the end they rot into dust in the same grave. All things are the same meaningless joke to me for they grin at me from one skull of death. (128)

He stands apart from and above the rest of humanity, represented in the play by the denizens of Hope's bar. As such, he is poet, visionary, philosopher and fool, articulating questions the others cannot begin to comprehend, undergoing an anguish to which the others are immune.

The other people in the bar, all having given up active and ambitious lives, pass their days in a drunken stupor reminiscing about the past and keeping alive their 'pipe-dreams' of what tomorrow may bring. It is the maintenance of these delusions that sustains them and keeps disillusion at bay. Like Mary Tyrone or Maggie Pollitt, they know that as long as they can hold on to a dream, they are saved.

Larry, believing that he himself is free of delusions, expatiates on the importance of dreams and life-lies:

> To hell with the truth! As the history of the world proves, the truth has no bearing on anything. It's irrelevant and immaterial as the lawyers say. The lie of a pipe dream is what gives life to the whole misbegotten lot of us, drunk or sober. (9–10)

As in *Cat on a Hot Tin Roof*, in *A Streetcar named Desire* and in *Long Day's Journey into Night*, only delusions can keep disillusion at bay. When the truth is faced and disillusion necessarily sets in, all hope is lost.

The threat of truth comes into the bar of illusions in the form of the salesman Theodore (God's beloved) Hickman, also known as 'Hickey'. Instead of joining in the celebration and drinking as is his custom on annual visits, he arrives bringing with him the gospel of peace. He surprises the people when he claims to have relinquished all illusions, thus reaching a state of peace, and urges them to do the same, for the truth shall set them free. He tells Larry that even his cynicism does not begin to compare with the nihilistic vision he is offering:

> You'll be grateful to me when all at once you find you're able to admit, without feeling ashamed, that all the grandstand

foolosopher bunk and the waiting for the Big Sleep stuff is a pipe dream. You'll say to yourself, I'm just an old man who is scared of life, but even more scared of dying. So I'm keeping drunk and hanging on to life at any price, and what of it? Then you'll know what real peace means, Larry, because you won't be scared of either life or death any more. You simply won't give a damn! Any more than I do! (116)

Hickey's message creates an immediate disturbance: several of the people make an unsuccessful attempt to leave the bar and face the outside world. Larry is quick to sense that Hickey has 'started a movement that'll blow up the world' (104), that this false Messiah with his message of nihilism has brought despair and thus death into the house of delusions.

In the course of the play the barflies find out that Hickey's faithful wife Evelyn is dead; only gradually do the circumstances surrounding her murder come to light. At the end of Act Two Hickey announces his wife's death; by the end of Act Three he discloses that she had been murdered; finally in Act Four he confesses to her murder. The fundamentalist Evelyn's boundless gift for forgiveness, her readiness to overlook her husband's transgressions, had made Hickey's life with her unbearable. Evelyn's faith in Hickey – her 'pipe-dream' as he calls it – only made the guilt feelings increasingly unbearable. To alleviate these feelings, Hickey had to break the cycle of transgression and forgiveness; following his own demented rationale, he killed Evelyn in order to bring peace to both of them.

Hickey finally admits to the relief he felt upon murdering Evelyn. When he realized that Evelyn would have forgiven him even this transgression, he heard himself say to her something he had always wanted to say. He recalls that he exclaimed: 'Well, you know what you can do with your pipe dream now, you damned bitch!' (242). Shocked and terrified by his own confession, he promptly denies what he had just said. Unable to face the fact that he hated Evelyn, he now insists on having killed her in a moment of insanity.

As Hickey proceeds with his lengthy confession the bar dwellers become more and more impatient when they realize that they are dealing with a deranged mind. All they want is to be left alone. Harry Hope voices their collective sentiment when he tells Hickey:

Get it over, you long-winded bastard! You married her, you caught her cheating with the iceman, and you croaked her, and

> who the hell cares? What's she to us? All we want is to pass out in peace, bejees! (234)

Their idea of peace and happiness is contingent on the perpetuation of their pipe dreams and on a state of intoxication. Finally they gain some solace from the conviction that they knew all along that Hickey was just 'a bughouse preacher escaped from an asylum' (244). They are now free once again to pass out in peace because any disturbance Hickey's new creed may have created was only temporary.

The roomers at Harry Hope's bar function as a chorus, an indistinguishable mass each member of which expresses his or her own variation upon the same theme. Only three characters are set apart from the rest: Hickey, the outsider who threatens to crush all hope, Don Parritt, the guilt-ridden police informer, and Larry Slade, former activist, thinker, commentator and 'Old Grandstand Foolosopher'. These three are distinguishable from the rest partly by their relationship to the truth and thus to death.

Hickey's gospel and his subsequent confession have the most dramatic effect on Don Parritt, who has just betrayed his anarchist mother – Larry's former lover – by turning her in to the police. His gradual self-revelation parallels Hickey's: first he claims to have betrayed the movement out of patriotic duty; later he admits to having done it for the money; finally, under the emotional impact of Hickey's admission of guilt, he admits that it was hatred of his mother that made him betray her. Parritt's horror at his moral transgression culminates in his suicide following Larry's urgings. His betrayal and his masking of hatred as idealism signal his entry into the fallen world. O'Neill is implying that political idealism usually deteriorates into (or perhaps is finally unmasked as) hatred, greed and malice. Parritt cannot face his shame at the loss of innocence. His confession may parrot[5] Hickey's, but in fact he stands at the very opposite end of the spectrum.

Hickey is despair and nihilism incarnate. He has come face to face with the void, and now he wishes to impose his vision on the others. Furthermore, his 'truth' turns out to be false. Dennis Welch, in 'Hickey as Satanic Force in *The Iceman Cometh*', goes so far as to say that Hickey is a Lucifer figure, an anti-Christ, a wolf in sheep's clothing. Indeed, Hickey insinuates himself into people's confidences as he embarks upon his mission of bringing to others the despair and nothingness he calls the truth. By killing Evelyn he has in effect murdered love and faith; he has taken away people's hope by urging them to embrace the 'truth' of hopelessness.

Larry Slade stands at the middle of this spectrum ranging from corrupted innocence to unmitigated cynicism. He is the only one at the bar who is aware of Parritt's suicide and both intellectually and emotionally affected by Hickey's visit. The others remain oblivious to the events after Hickey is removed by the police and ignorant of Larry's insight, singing their individual songs as the play ends in a cacophony of tunes.

In this play, each new truth turns out to be false and every certainty the characters may harbor just another illusion. Even Larry's pose of philosophical detachment and of misanthropic cynicism proves to be a form of self-delusion. James Cameron, 'Jimmy Tomorrow', sees through the 'Old Foolosopher' from the start when he says to him: 'No, Larry, old friend, you can't deceive me. You pretend a bitter, cynic philosophy, but in your heart you are the kindest man among us' (44). Larry has both the darkest vision of humanity and the greatest pity for its follies. His final speech best sums up the irreconcilable conflicts he experiences upon Parritt's suicide and the irony with which he views his own situation:

> (*in a whisper of horrified pity*) Poor devil! (*A long-forgotten faith returns to him for a moment and he mumbles*) God rest his soul in peace. (*He opens his eyes – with a bitter self-derision*) Ah, the damned pity – the wrong kind, as Hickey said! Be God, there's no hope! I'll never be a success in the grandstand – or anywhere else! Life is too much for me! I'll be a weak fool looking with pity at the two sides of everything till the day I die! (*With an intense bitter sincerity*) May that day come soon! (*He pauses startedly, surprised at himself – then with a sardonic grin*) Be God, I'm the only real convert to death Hickey made here. From the bottom of my coward's heart I mean that now! (258)

As the curtain falls, Larry remains *'in his chair by the window'*, apart from the group, *'oblivious to their racket'* (260) and staring in front of him. As observer, dilettante philosopher and fool, Larry is forever poised above the others, and even above himself, due to excessive awareness and an overly analytical mind.

His self-awareness and self-vigilance mark him as a tragic hero of sorts. In 'The Wisdom of Silenus in O'Neill's *Iceman*', William Brashear interprets the play in Nietzschean terms and argues that

Larry embodies the tragic Dionysian/Apollonian duality. Hence Larry is conscious of the internal balance between a Dionysian awareness of chaos – leading to despair – and the Apollonian impulse to resist despair through the creation of illusion. Perpetually examining all sides of the question, Larry is like Hamlet in his inability to act, Brashear points out. Brashear is right that Larry shares Hamlet's indecisiveness, but there the comparison ends: in the universe of Harry Hope's bar, Larry is the final arbiter. The joke may be on him, and he may be a fool, but there is no viable alternative to his insight. In this sense, of course, the comparison with Hamlet is not only superficial but also essentially misguided since it does not account for the play's pessimistic view of life. The only alternative to Larry's anguished dual vision is the blindness of the rest of the people in the bar. They have only the limited perspective of their pipe-dreams and are immobilized by the power of their own delusions. When the iceman – death in the person of Hickey – appears, they mistake him for the bridegroom – redemption. Only Larry knows that death has come into their midst. There is no clear resolution here. The roomers remain numbed by alcohol, deluded by their pipe dreams; Larry remains condemned to tragic insight. Similarly, at the end of *Long Day's Journey into Night* the Tyrones are unchanged, struggling to cling onto their pipe-dreams and escape intolerable insight through intoxication. In *The Iceman Cometh* and *Long Day's Journey into Night* survival – usually expressed in terms of endurance – has to do with a persistent struggle against the intrusions of reality into the anguished life of the conscience.

In *Cat on a Hot Tin Roof* survival is dramatized in both biological and psychological terms as Williams explores physical and spiritual survival on several levels; personal, familial, societal, existential. The main action involves questions of inheritance and revolves around the problem of transfer of power within the family. However, Brick's paralysis, Big Daddy's uremic condition and Maggie's infertility and frustrated sexual desire must be seen, as Williams indicates, in all their far-reaching implications.

Big Daddy, patriarch and owner of 'twenty-eight thousand acres of the richest land this side of the valley Nile' (65), stands at the centre of the play. In the original, published version – Williams' favourite[6] – Big Daddy makes his impressive appearance in Act Two and does not reappear. As Williams indicates in his 'Note of Explanation' and in his *Memoirs*, the director Elia Kazan wanted to make Maggie more admirable, to bring back Big Daddy in Act Three, and to have Brick change his stance in the course of the play. Williams reluctantly agreed to the first change for he found Maggie to be a positive character and wanted audiences to see her that way. He also brought back Big Daddy in the last act. However, he felt convinced that Brick simply could not undergo any transformation requested by Kazan. He was skeptical of the possibility of any marked change in Brick's beliefs or behavior. In the 'Note of Explanation' he writes:

> I felt that the moral paralysis of Brick was a root thing in his tragedy, and to show a dramatic progression would obscure the meaning of that tragedy in him . . . I don't believe that a conversation, however revelatory, ever effects so immediate a change in the heart or even conduct of a person in Brick's state of spiritual disrepair. (125)

Although he made these changes for the Broadway production, he subsequently considered the new version a disaster (*Memoirs*, 169).[7]

It would be difficult to declare one character in the play the protagonist. Maggie, Brick and Big Daddy seem to share this role. Maggie's battle gives the play its title; Brick's paralysis emblematizes the condition of impasse, and Big Daddy's vitality symbolizes life – and therefore also degeneration and death – and provides the contextual dimension. The three characters represent three aspects of existence: Big Daddy the material, Blanche the physical and Brick the spiritual. Williams sympathizes with Maggie's passionate struggle to regain Brick's love. On the other hand, Brick may be seen as the central tragic figure and, in fact, Williams describes him in those terms. It should also not be overlooked that Williams uses the last stanza of Dylan Thomas' 'Do Not Go Gentle into That Good Night' as an epigraph for the play and that Big Daddy's declamations about the darker side of human nature and about mortality represent a desperate last effort to 'rage against the dying of the light'. Clearly, the father's bout with death constitutes as significant a theme as Maggie's 'victory of a cat on a hot tin roof' (or 'a cat on hot *bricks*', as the saying goes) or Brick's disgust with mendacity.

In more ways than one, both in terms of the inheritance and in terms of thematic relevance, Maggie stands between Brick and Big Daddy. More manipulative and less ferocious than her father-in-law, she nonetheless shares his survival instinct. She may even be construed as a female version of Big Daddy. She is the unmistakably sexual feline whose greatest accomplishment is survival through manipulation, compromise and adaptation. If Brick stands for the 'charm of the defeated' and Big Daddy for life in all its crudeness and cruelty, Maggie stands not only for sexual greed but in her own manner also for the sustenance of dreams and for hope. After all, for better or worse, only she can make 'a Little Father' of Brick. Although Big Daddy strikes an unsympathetic response in many readers/viewers, Williams maintains in his *Memoirs* that he was impressed with the patriarch's 'crude eloquence of expression' (168) and describes Big Daddy as having 'kingly magnitude' (235). In terms of dramatic power, the patriarch is more dynamic, and therefore more interesting, than Brick who may have our sympathies. Finally, both Big Daddy's clinging to life and Brick's courting of death are essential to Williams' theme of duality, as is Maggie's fundamental desire for sexual fulfilment, procreation and inheritance. Maggie's sexual and material yearnings have their equivalent in Big Daddy's love of property.

Big Daddy is not only large and grand: he is an embodiment of uncontrolled growth, one of the key images in the play and a polar opposite to the sterile Brick. After having worked hard in the fields and having become an overseer, he took over the plantation and, as he says, 'the place got bigger and bigger and bigger and bigger and bigger!' (61). He continues to be amazed about the phenomenon of accumulation and growth. He tells Brick:

> You git you a piece of land, by hook or crook, an'things start growin' on it, things accumulate on it, and the first thing you know it's completely out of hand, completely out of hand! (61)

Uncontrolled growth in all its forms – accumulation of wealth, excessive fertility, cancer, even cumulative language – characterizes all the Pollitts, with the exception of Brick. In particular, in his expatiations on human nature Big Daddy revels in repetitious, incremental rhythmical language. In Act Two, for instance, he repeats the resounding lines:

> the human animal is a selfish beast (65)
> the human animal is a beast that dies (66)
> the human animal is a beast that dies and if he's got

money he buys and buys and buys (67)

These proverbial utterances succinctly sum up human nature for Big Daddy. According to the patriarch, humanity's chief character traits and main motivating forces are greed, egoism and fear of mortality; all these forces drive Big Daddy.

An excrescent condition, as well as the crudest form of materialism, is most comically exemplified by Big Daddy's son Gooper and his family. The lawyer Gooper and his pregnant wife Mae, with their brood of 'no-neck monsters', not only stand for conventional family life as Williams' comic eye sees it, but are also a grotesque caricature of rapacious survivors. Like birds of prey, they descend upon Big Daddy's estate hoping to gain advantage over childless Brick and Maggie. They are potential guardians of Big Daddy's wealth and perpetuators of his way of life. It is through them that the life cycle can continue and the future be ensured. And it is to this future that Brick refuses to give his approval.

Brick has in effect opted out of life. This is the nature of his paralyzing idealism: having lost the one pure and meaningful thing – his friendship with Skipper – he has given up the fight. He now has the *'charm of that cool air of detachment that people have who have given up the struggle'* (stage directions, 17). However, *'at some deeper level he is far from peaceful'*, and it is this restlessness that the conversation with Big Daddy in Act Two brings to the surface. Like the Tyrone brothers, Brick drinks in order to preserve his detachment. He tells Big Daddy that he drinks in order to kill his disgust with 'mendacity' which pervades all relationships and dominates all human transactions, just as greed motivates them. Unwilling to participate in this mendacious system, he drinks till he hears the 'click' that signals peace of mind or oblivion.

Big Daddy, on the other hand, has made his wealth by living the lie. He knows not only that he has had to live with mendacity all his life, but also that 'there's nothing *else* to *live* with except mendacity' (81). Therefore he urges Brick to learn to live with it. Having faced death, he has attained a level of understanding that is not within Brick's reach. Big Daddy is now disgusted by hypocrisy and greed, tormented by thoughts of mortality. At a point in the play when he does not know that he is dying, he comments that 'the human animal is a beast that dies but the fact that he's dying don't give him pity for others' (66). This sums up Big Daddy's situation, unbeknownst to him.

Although in this play, just as in *All My Sons* and to some extent in *Death of a Salesman,* typologically speaking, the father represents mendacity and the son veracity, in fact Big Daddy has truthful insights and Brick's vision is clouded by his own untruthfulness. Indeed, the irony of Brick's situation is that his disgust with mendacity is in fact rooted in his denial of the one true friendship he had experienced – the relationship with Skipper. As Williams says, this *'may be the root of his collapse. Or maybe it is only a single manifestation of it, not even the most important'* (85). Brick's paralysis is partly a result of having denied a homosexual relationship which could not be faced because of Brick's bowing to contemporary societal standards.

There is a special understanding between the father who is dying but embracing life to the fullest and the son who is in the prime of life but almost not alive. Indeed, the powerful Big Daddy becomes not only confessor to but also spokesman for the distressed and taciturn Brick. In Act Two father and son confront one another in an exercise in unmasking. Big Daddy is able to break through Brick's detachment and expose it for the posturing it is. He reminds his son that his alcoholism dates back to his friend Skipper's death. In fact, Big Daddy blames Brick for Skipper's death (Brick had shunned his friend fearing his possible homosexuality) and sees this act of betrayal as the real motivation for his son's detachment: 'This disgust with mendacity is disgust with yourself. *You*! – dug the grave of your friend and kicked him in it! – before you'd face truth with him!' (92). When Big Daddy penetrates Brick's mask of aloofness and exposes his mendacity, Brick decides to punish him for this destructive insight. To avenge himself, he tells Big Daddy the truth about his physical condition; he tells him that he is dying of cancer.

When his father's face *'crumbles like broken yellow plaster about to fall into dust'* (94), Brick apologizes:

> I'm sorry, Big Daddy. My head don't work any more and it's hard for me to understand how anybody could care if he lived or died or was dying or cared about anything but whether or not there was liquor left in the bottle and so I said what I said without thinking. (94)

Like Chris Keller in *All My Sons,* Brick forces the truth upon his father. However, here the truth which brings death is not a sign of idealism but only a cruel act of revenge. Big Daddy's reaction is one of shock and revulsion; he is now disgusted with the doctors' and his family's mendacity.

It had been a comfort to Big Daddy that he had not been aware of his approaching death. As he points out, human beings are the only animals who have awareness of their own mortality. And this is a disadvantage, for 'Ignorance – of mortality – is a comfort . . . The others go without knowing . . . without any knowledge of it, and yet a pig squeals, but a man sometimes, he can keep a tight mouth about it' (68). In Act Three the absent Big Daddy squeals like a pig, fully cognizant not only of mortality, but of his own imminent death as well. His presence makes itself known as an off-stage *'long drawn cry of agony and rage'* (120).

In *Cat on a Hot Tin Roof,* as in *Long Day's Journey into Night* and in *The Iceman Cometh,* truth and death are closely allied, as are mendacity and life. In varying degrees, the self-appointed heralds of truth often turn out to be heralds of death. Brick sees himself as truthful and not fully alive: 'In some ways I'm no better than the others, in some ways worse because I'm less alive. Maybe it's being alive that makes them lie, and being almost *not* alive makes me sort of accidentally truthful . . . ' (94). As in *The Wild Duck,* it is the 'mendacity', the 'pipe dream', that gives life. Believing in the possibility of his recovery gives Big Daddy life. The truth about his death reduces him to an off-stage cry. Not facing his own mendacity sustains Brick in his self-righteous condemnation of the mendacity of others.

Maggie's life-giving lie – that she is pregnant with Brick's baby – promises to make a 'Little Father' out of Brick and endow Big Daddy with immortality by continuing the life cycle. With the help of this lie Maggie, the cat of the title, is determined to win over Mae. More subtle in her fortune hunting than her openly rapacious sister-in-law, she hopes to win back her husband in order to get her hands on Big Daddy's money. Unlike Brick, she is not ready to give up and lives for the hope that one day Brick will come back to her. She describes herself as a survivor:

> . . . one thing I don't have is the charm of the defeated, my hat is still in the ring, and I am determined to win! . . . – What is the victory of a cat on a hot tin roof? – I wish I knew . . . . just staying on it, I guess, as long as she can . . . . (25)

Perseverance, the sustaining of illusions, is the mark of Maggie's tenacious heroism.

She believes she had lost Brick and destroyed Skipper when she confronted them with the truth concerning their relationship. She had ordered Skipper to stop loving her husband, and when Skipper ran away, she sought him out:

> When I came to his room that night, with a little scratch like a shy little mouse at his door, he made that pitiful, ineffectual little attempt to prove that what I had said wasn't true . . – In this way, I destroyed him by telling him truth that he and his world which he was born and raised in, yours and his world, had told him could not be told? (45)

The revelation of this truth has the same effect as the similar confrontation has in *A Streetcar Named Desire.* In both cases what is called the truth by Maggie and by Blanche is in fact the societal lie. Brick's betrayal of Skipper is tantamount to his having chosen this societal mendacity over the private truth.

Brick believes that not love with Maggie but 'friendship with Skipper was that one great true thing' (44). 'It was', he says 'too rare to be normal, any true thing between two people is too rare to be normal' (89). The Skipper/Brick relationship, unlike the Maggie/Brick one, does not involve procreation and does not partake of the life-cycle presided over by the patriarchial Big Daddy. In a sense, because it is not subject to this regeneration, it is also oblivious to degeneration and to death.

Maggie's mendacious announcement is meant to remedy the destructive veracities of the past. In the end Maggie seems to have victory on her side. She locks up Brick's liquor and announces triumphantly: 'And so tonight we're going to make the lie true, and when that's done, I'll bring the liquor back here and we'll get drunk together, here, tonight, in this place that death has come into . . . .' (123). The play is open-ended, but it seems unlikely – except in the Broadway version – that Maggie will win back Brick. The death that has come into the Pollitt house is not just Big Daddy's death but, more significantly, also the death of the spirit. When Maggie confesses her love for Brick, he answers by repeating the words Big Daddy mutters (59) when Big Mamma confesses her love for him: 'Wouldn't it be funny if that was true?' (123). The statement may be construed as an omen: perhaps one day Brick will emulate Big

Daddy and will live his lie. However, the phrase also echoes the closing lines in *The Sun Also Rises*, a conversation between Jake Barnes – like Brick, physically and spiritually wounded – and Brett:

> 'Oh, Jake', Brett said, 'we could have had such a damned good time together'. . . . 'Yes', I said. 'Isn't it pretty to think so?'

The lack of resolution in *Cat on a Hot Tin Roof* may be attributed to Williams' skepticism concerning the possibility of a satisfactory breaking of the deadlock and of a successful resolution of the conflict. In structural terms, the play dramatizes an irreconcilable conflict and a balance of views rather than a conclusive resolution. In the universe of the play, the world is shown to be unworthy, and yet the need for struggle is also demonstrated. Brick's resignation is not offered as the answer, but neither are Maggie's or Big Daddy's responses.

Like Jake Barnes' injury in *The Sun Also Rises*, Brick's crisis of conscience, his debilitating spiritual injury – symbolized by the broken ankle and sexual impotence – must be seen as a single instance in the general crisis. Brick's state, as he understands it, is a response to the spiritual ruin embodied by Big Daddy whose uremic condition is a symptom of a state of physical and moral degeneration and decay.

Mendacity, the overt subject of the play, is one of the forms (brutal veracity is the other) betrayal takes. Brick claims that he is rejecting mendacity, but in fact he is dodging life because he cannot face his own act of betrayal. In *The Iceman Cometh*, in *Long Day's Journey into Night* and in *Cat on a Hot Tin Roof* the truth is shown to be largely inaccessible, possibly dangerous for most people and immaterial even when penetrated by few exceptional individuals. As Brick puts it, 'mendacity is a system that we live in. Liquor is one way out an' death's the other' (94). This sentiment is certainly shared by the characters in *The Iceman Cometh* and in *Long Day's Journey into Night*, all of whom consider the solace of alcoholic escape an apt alternative to the eternal sleep.

In the two O'Neill plays, as well as in *Cat on a Hot Tin Roof*, the characters are trapped in their situations, doomed to play out the same scenes over and over again. Genuine faith and idealism are no longer the issues here: 'staying on', resisting despair, and refusing to relinquish the life-sustaining lies take the place of the

> the thwarted desire of people to reach others through this fog, this screen of incomprehension. (Devlin, 40)

In this view the desire for the continuation of life is brought into heroic conflict with the competing death-wish. In *Cat on a Hot Tin Roof*, for instance, the existential conflict between the life-force and the death-wish is played out by Brick and Big Daddy. Similarly, in *Long Day's Journey into Night* individual characters are torn between the two conflicting desires. In these plays, incomprehension, loneliness, alienation and suffering are normative; they are not contingent on a specific action or dependent on an extraordinary character.

The view of life represented in *Cat on a Hot Tin Roof*, *Long Day's Journey into Night* and *The Iceman Cometh* shares a pessimism espoused, among others, by Dowson and other symbolist poets as well as by Schopenhauer, one of Jamie Tyrone's intellectual idols. According to the philosopher, tragedy reflects the worthlessness of individual life. The goal of tragedy is to show 'the unspeakable pain, the wail of humanity, the triumph of evil, the scornful mastery of chance and the irretrievable fall of the just and the innocent'. In this scheme the hero atones not for individual sins or transgressions but for original sin, for the sin of existence. Therefore, the best kind of tragedy, Schopenhauer believes, shows 'characters of ordinary morality, under circumstances such as often occur . . . doing each other greatest injury, without any one of them being entirely in the wrong' (*The World as Will and Idea*). Such is the fate of the characters in *Long Day's Journey into Night* who are doomed to torment each other for the rest of their lives. Jamie Tyrone's, Big Daddy's and Larry Slade's dark views of existence and of human nature also echo the Schopenhauerian belief in universal injustice.

In the midst of this pessimistic vision, however, Williams and Miller insist on a positive note: just as an overwhelming feeling of guilt accompanies the characters on their journeys, they are motivated by the need to transcend guilt and to forgive themselves and others. In the two family plays, a need for love and understanding mitigates the hostilities; similarly, the shared fate of the denizens of Harry Hope's bar renders existence tolerable. In final analysis, the struggle for survival in these plays is heroic because, as Larry Slade's situation so appropriately shows, it reveals the darkest vision, accompanied by a death-wish, and also involves a painful recognition of a need for continuity, represented by the life-force.

Conclusion

Miller, Williams, O'Neill and Anderson not only do not provide a systematic theory of tragedy, they frequently do not engage in an easily classifiable dramatic practice. They often ignore the formal aspects and the philosophical dimension of traditional tragedy, and instead focus on its intensified character portrayal which they believe typifies the genre. They identify tragedy with dramatization of heroism and invariably define it in terms of the protagonist's idealistic dedication to a cause and his or her subsequent suffering. Thus they redefine tragedy as primarily a dramatic tribute to individualism and to human potential.

O'Neill and Anderson maintain that because traditional tragedy recognizes and celebrates human greatness and dignity, tragic drama on the modern stage has a potential for glorifying a diminished humanity and affirming an optimistic view of existence. Indeed, for each playwright, tragedy, as he defines it, offers proof of a particular aspect of human dignity. For Anderson and Miller tragedy affirms a liberal humanist vision of the world with its faith in social ameliorism and moral progress. For O'Neill, whose apparent pessimism in the late plays is engendered by a yearning for an optimistic vision, tragedy provides an intensified, often mystical, view of the essential struggle and suffering of life which gives protagonists dignity. For Williams tragedy offers a dramatic expression of the romantic yearning for timelessness approximated by means of an aesthetic arrest of time. In several of his plays the essentially tragic condition of humanity is shown to be a function of its mortality; tragedy chronicles the ennobling struggle against time.

Miller's belief that tragedy will show humanity 'the right way to live in the world', Anderson's faith in gradual betterment of the 'race' and O'Neill's vision of a Nietzschean spiritual super-man all indicate the moral mandate these playwrights assign to tragedy and to heroism. Their interest in tragedy often grows out of a very strong desire for order and faith as well as for an unfragmented aesthetic tradition. In varying degrees, Miller, Williams, Anderson and O'Neill see their own age as having lost not only religious faith but also faith in human worth, and they consider modern skepticism as an obstacle to the creation of tragedy and dramatization of heroism. Tragedy presupposes not only a fatalistic vision (which these playwrights often modify and redefine) but also spiritual grandeur and faith in human dignity; by contrast, with the possible exception of Miller, they believe that the modern age is essentially rationalistic, non-fatalistic and skeptical.

Their approach to character and their attraction to tragedy are founded on a suspicion of rationalism. However, they no longer seem to draw the Nietzschean equation between rationalism and anti-tragic optimism but rather between rationalism and anti-tragic pessimism. As Camus pointed out in 'The Future of Tragedy', disillusionment with rationalism, or rather skepticism regarding rationalism as a panacea for humanity's ills, is responsible for an all-pervasive pessimism, specifically for the perception of the diminished stature of humanity, both in life and on the stage, as well as for a new type of fatalism. Anderson repeatedly blames science, scientific progress and rationalism for all the evils of the world. Similarly, O'Neill considers the spiritual poverty of modern life and its destructive materialism to be a result of the victory of rationalism. Although Williams makes no such explicit statement against rationalism, his morally and spiritually superior protagonists represent anti-rational lyrical sensibility and poetic sentiment in opposition to a materialistic, non-heroic and essentially rational world.

In these dramas of character, protagonists cannot hope to achieve greatness or wield significant power; the most they can hope for is to preserve their integrity and to maintain their dignity. Even in Miller's early 'social' plays, such as *All My Sons, Death of a Salesman* and *The Crucible*, the preservation of integrity is the main issue. For instance, in Chris Keller's quest for the truth, individualistic self-righteousness rather than social idealism seems to be the motive. As a consequence, the maintenance of individuality is a recurring theme in these plays. The playwrights' ideas of individualism bear some similarity to the romantic liberal ideas that Lukács, in 'The Sociology of Modern Drama', describes operating in German drama of the nineteenth and early twentieth century and having their roots in Romanticism. As Lukács maintains:

> The realization and maintenance of personality has become on the one hand a conscious problem of living; the longing to make

> the personality prevail grows increasingly pressing and urgent. On the other hand, external circumstances, which rule out this possibility from the first, gain even greater weight. It is in this way that survival as an individual, the integrity of individuality, becomes the vital centre of drama. Indeed the bare fact of Being begins to turn tragic. (Bentley, 1976, 433)

Lukács contends that individualism at the turn of the century is 'conscious and problematic' (432); therefore, tragedy results from 'the mere realization of personality' (433) because 'where tragedy was previously brought on by the particular *direction* taken by the will, the mere *act* of willing suffices to induce it in the new tragedy' (433). The preoccupation with the maintenance of individual integrity figures in all the categories of heroism discussed here. In the plays in Chapter 2 (Idealism as Heroism) and in Chapter 3 (Martyrdom as Heroism) the protagonists risk their sanity and their lives in order to preserve their integrity. Proctor, in *The Crucible,* sacrifices everything for his 'name'; Willy Loman kills himself to prove to Biff that he is worth more than 'a dime a dozen'. In Chapter 5 (Survival as Heroism), survival in terms of simply existing is contingent on the maintenance of individual dignity. In a somewhat different vein, in the plays discussed in Chapter 4 (Self-reflection as Heroism), the external world is presented in terms of individual perception, and extreme alienating individualism becomes problematic as it verges on solipsism.

If there is a prevalent belief system in these plays, it is in the primacy of individual integrity over collective standards. Especially in Williams' plays, the norms of the herd – represented by such figures as Stanley Kowalski in *A Streetcar Named Desire* and the mob in *Orpheus Descending* – or the ideals of bourgeois decency – embodied in such diverse figures as Amanda Wingfield, the Goopers and Stella Kowalski – are shunned by the protagonists who must, like all 'fugitive kind', always remain outsiders. The heroic individual is the final moral arbiter and the spokesperson for the playwrights' individualistic ideals. Unlike Greek or Elizabethan tragedies, these plays do not indicate the presence of a larger moral framework that the protagonist must abide by or perish. The standards of the society are repeatedly shown to be unethical and/or inadequate for individual expression. Therefore the protagonists establish their own acceptable standards, and it is by these that they are judged and they judge themselves.

Preservation of moral integrity seems to be the most admirable aim of these modern protagonists who must endure suffering in order to retain some semblance of self-esteem and to remain true to their beliefs. George Lukács's observations, in 'The Sociology of Modern Drama', on the ambivalent and problematic nature of modern individualism may once again be recalled here. Lukács distinguishes between drama of great individuals (or Renaissance drama) and drama of individualism (or bourgeois Romantic drama). Lukács is referring primarily to German dramatists such as Schiller, Goethe, Grabbe and Lenz who dramatized the problematic nature of individualism in an era of rationalism and changing economic relations. It is the modern awareness of the impossibility of writing drama of great individuals that engenders the drama of individualism. The main difference in terms of the role of the individual is that

> the old drama, by which we mean here primarily that of the Renaissance, was drama of great individuals, today's is that of individualism. In other words, the realization of personality, its *per se* expression in life, could in no wise become a theme of earlier drama, since personality was not yet problematic. It is, in the drama of today, the chief and most central problem. (433)

The modern era is characterized by both uniformity and individualist tendencies, Lukács asserts. At such times, the drama focuses on small protagonists' attempts to distinguish themselves from the uniform mass of humanity and to retain their identity and integrity. For instance, in *Death of a Salesman* Willy, like numerous other protagonists, wishes both to reassert his uniqueness and to be part of the collective. It is precisely this tension between uniformity and individualism, between community membership and private isolation that the plays discussed here echo. Due to the lack of a larger moral and metaphysical order, the protagonist is usually surrounded by the corrupt society consisting of fallen individuals. He or she has the choice of being part of this reprehensible community or perishing alone. The tension between 'belonging' and standing apart is central to all the plays and seems to concern all four playwrights.

In keeping with the tenets of this form of romanticism, the prerequisite for heroism seems to be the total alienation from the general population. This takes the form not of banishment but of self-imposed exile and estrangement. Whereas the classical or Elizabethan tragic hero usually ends in exile, separated from the community, the protagonists of these American plays begin in exile. They are outsiders from the outset. While not belonging and being a perpetual outsider are the characteristics of the hero or the heroine, the struggle to re-familiarize and reintegrate is also the source of heroic anguish and of tragic consequence. Miller's plays in particular seem to contend that the more private people become and the more separate from the society of which they are both product and producer, the greater their estrangement and sense of loss. They both abandon society and are abandoned by it. In O'Neill's plays the quest for belonging is a response to a different kind of 'abandonment' and has to do with the search for God. In *After the Fall*, Miller's focus shifts from social abandonment to existential abandonment as he dramatizes Quentin's search for meaning and for judgement.

Two fundamentally different dramatic approaches to the modern condition can be distinguished here. First, the attempt to remedy social alienation and psychic fragmentation – caused by the split between individual desire and social cause – by showing people in the social context and second, the attempt to remedy the loss of individuality and of personal integrity – caused by the subsumption of the individual in the social machine – by stressing people's inner selves and their spiritual lives. Both the movement outward, away from the inner self and toward a reintegration into society, and the movement inward, into an exploration of the self, can partake of an intensity which is heroic and tragic. In the plays of Miller, Williams, Anderson and O'Neill, protagonists struggle with these conflicting tendencies as they are torn between exclusive allegiance to self and to other.

Many of the protagonists in the plays under discussion are guilty of a moral transgression, of a betrayal of their own individual standards and thus of a truth which the community does not necessarily share. In some of the plays, most markedly in those discussed in Chapter 5, the facing of one's own truth requires great courage and is often associated with death. Only through the cultivation of illusions, 'pipe-dreams', 'mendacity', – or beauty, magic and art, as Blanche DuBois might call them – is existence made tolerable and the desired return to innocence, both private and public, made possible.

Heroism seems to be repeatedly equated with intensity, whether in terms of idealism or feeling. Excesses of feeling – not necessarily acted upon – are often the mark of the heroic self-divided protagonist. In this re-emergence of romanticism, which Miller decried but of which he was a part, the social environment is often a reflection of the hero's psyche, that is, its reality is established in terms of the hero's perceptions. The presence of this intensity also answers the question of heroic stature as it provides what social standing and intellectual superiority are no longer expected to: a nobility which has to do with potential for intense feeling and with willingness to undergo suffering. Heroism is redefined to include feeling and thought rather than action, and intellectual, emotional and spiritual nobility now take the place of nobility of deeds.

In the now famous 1949 conversations with Georges Duthuit, Beckett described the function of contemporary art as an 'expression that there is nothing to express, nothing with which to express, no desire to express, together with the obligation to express'. In the diverse plays that I examined in this book, the protagonists fear and suspect that there may be nothing to express, but their desire to express it takes them into a heroic spheres. They function in a pre-Beckettian universe where nihilism is not yet a given and heroism is still an attainable objective, and within an aesthetic framework that only *describes* a loss of meaning – in some cases only admits to its possibility – but does not always *subscribe* to it.

In their dedication to writing meaningful contemporary tragedies and dramatizing modern heroism, Miller, Williams, O'Neill and Anderson reveal a 'desire to express'. In the larger context of modern drama, their redefinitions of heroism are the last attempts to find that 'with which to express'. This is not to suggest that with Beckett modern drama has reached a point of no return or that his statement accounts for all of serious drama in the second half of the century. After all, Beckett stands at the forefront of only one of several twentieth-century movements. However, the relentless attempts of modern dramatists to write tragedies and define heroism in a non-tragic, non-heroic age share the rhetorical spirit of Beckett's statement. Their superimposition of a traditional form – or of its remains – on modern content is just one instance of using the inherent value of the art form, in this case the tragic genre and accompanying concepts of heroism, to counterbalance a supposed lack of meaning in the subject matter.

Beckett's affirmatively nihilist statement is based on the understanding that as long as one can dramatize 'nothing' it must be something, that the very word 'obligation' denies any claims of amorality and absurdity. As long as playwrights can describe, as Miller has done, 'searching for a long time for a tragic hero' (*Timebends*, 342), or refer to the heroism of a character like Blanche DuBois, one may legitimately speak of redefinitions of heroism long after we have forgotten what was meant by the term in earlier forms of drama that speak to a different listener and play to a different audience.

Notes

INTRODUCTION

1. Miller documents in his recent autobiography, *Timebends*, that although in the thirties he thought of Odets as the only revolutionary American playwright and of O'Neill as 'the playwright of the mystical rich, high society and the Theatre Guild and escapist "culture"', in the forties he had come to think of him differently and upon seeing *The Iceman Cometh* was 'struck by O'Neill's radical hostility to bourgeois civilization, far greater than anything Odets had expressed' (228).

CHAPTER 1 HEROISM RECONSIDERED

1. Krutch was a great admirer and champion of O'Neill and contributed an introduction to the playwright's *Nine Plays*. Anderson's views on the modern age bear a strong resemblance to those of Krutch in *The Modern Temper* and elsewhere.
2. Kazin's *On Native Grounds* rather appropriately refers to Krutch's brand of criticism as 'self-consciously aristocratic and unwittingly sentimental' and argues that the 'very animus of Krutch's essay was to bolster the provincial superiority of the intellectuals by proving the universal inferiority of human life' (272).
3. Williams writes in his *Memoirs* that he *is* Blanche and it is also from this source that one knows that there was a real Stanley Kowalski to whom the playwright was sexually attracted. Although the validity of such superimpositions of this and other extraneous information on the play is questionable, awareness of these autobiographical details, specifically Williams' identification with the heroine, his ironic self-deprecation, his identification with and attraction to Stanley and, more importantly, to everything he represents, at least makes one doubt the many schematized critical views of the play.
4. Even when historical and political events figure in the plays – for instance the Spanish Civil War and the Depression in *The Glass Menagerie* – the focus is on the emotional impact they have on the characters rather than on the events themselves.
5. According to Sheaffer's biography, *O'Neill: Son and Playwright* (1968), O'Neill considered Nietzsche his literary idol and believed that *Thus Spake Zarathustra* had something to say 'to the homeless soul in search of a new faith' (123). He read this work of Nietzsche in the original with the help of a dictionary (304).

6. *The Ghost Sonata* in some more recent translations, for instance Sprigge's.
7. This almost limitless faith in the power of the theatre to inspire, educate and mold is curious, especially given the secondary status of theatre in American cultural life. References to 'the race' and to the visionary nature of drama are difficult to take seriously.

CHAPTER 2 IDEALISM AS HEROISM

1. Since the pagination in *Eleven Verse Plays* is not consecutive, quotations from different plays in the collection may appear to be on the same page.
2. When the idealistic Mary of Anderson's *Mary of Scotland* (1933) is defeated by the Machiavellian Elizabeth, she appeals to posterity and to an ultimate moral victory: 'In myself/ I know you to be an eater of dust/ . . . still, STILL I win! I have been/ A woman, and I have loved as a woman loves,/ Lost as a woman loses'. Mary's appeal – like Essex's – is to personal integrity.
3. *Inside his Head* was the title Miller originally intended for the play.

CHAPTER 3 MARTYRDOM AS HEROISM

1. Of the few critics who have dealt with the concept of 'the secret cause', Richard Sewall (*The Vision of Tragedy*, 1959) uses it to refer to a sense of mystery and terror; Normand Berlin (*The Secret Cause. A Discussion of Tragedy*, 1981) identifies it with the unknown, with any sense of mystery which he considers to constitute the essence of the tragic experience and the main criterion for tragedy. Accordingly, he classifies *Waiting for Godot* as a tragedy (it has a dimension of mystery), but dismisses *Death of a Salesman* (it lacks entirely in mystery). Presumably, what Berlin must mean by mystery is a metaphysical concern.

CHAPTER 4 SELF-REFLECTION AS HEROISM

1. O'Neill insisted that in writing *The Emperor Jones* and *The Hairy Ape* he was not influenced by German expressionism (Clark, 1924, 124–5). He believed he always attempted 'to find balance' between showing people as types and as individuals (Törnqvist, 1969, 31–2). Nonetheless, critics such as Blackburn and Valgemae (*Accelerated Grimace*, 1972) have studied the influence of Kaiser on O'Neill's theatre. In a letter written in 1930 to Robert Sisk, O'Neill discussed the effective blend of expressionism and naturalism in *The Hairy Ape* (Törnqvist, 32).

2. One could of course argue that Williams often managed to maintain an ironic distance from himself through writing and that the various 'autobiographical' figures or composites he created were ironic masks of the Williams persona.

CHAPTER 5 SURVIVAL AS HEROISM

1. The play was written in 1939, first performed and published in 1946.
2. The play was finished in 1940 but was not performed or published until 1956.
3. The 1955 Signet edition I am using contains both the original version and the Broadway version of Act Three, as well as Williams' 'Note of Explanation'. I believe that the 1974 substantially revised edition is inferior to the original 1955 version. In an attempt to make explicit the homosexual theme, Williams lost in both poetic and thematic subtlety what he gained in supposed openness. Rather than a more honest play, what emerges is an overwritten text where many of the non-sexual elements and those sexual elements which have a wider thematic function fade into the background and are, in all but exceptionally well-conceived performances, lost on the audience. The play is more overtly sexual, and consequently sensational; its conception is much narrower than that of the 1955 original.
4. The play equates homosexuality – or more precisely repressed homosexuality – with sterility. Although the bourgeois concept of family, especially its economic basis, is held up to ridicule, Brick must be viewed in the context of the environment into which the playwright places him and within which he is expected to function, and thus necessarily be seen as deficient. Like Jake Barnes in *The Sun Also Rises*, he just does not measure up.
5. Much has been made of the parrot/Parritt pun.
6. The published version of the play was not only his preferred one but, moreover, the favorite of all his plays because of its Aristotelian unity of time and place and its magnitude of theme (*Memoirs*, 168).
7. See my note on the three versions of the play.

Bibliography

Abel, Lionel. *Metatheatre. A New View of Dramatic Form*. New York: Hill and Wang, 1963.

Adler, Thomas P. *Mirror on the Stage. The Pulitzer Plays as an Approach to American Drama*. West Lafayette, Ind.: Purdue University Press, 1987.

——. 'The Search for God in the Plays of Tennessee Williams'. *Renascence* 26 (Autumn 1973): 48–56. Stanton 138–48.

Alexander, Doris M. 'Hugo of *The Iceman Cometh*: Realism and O'Neill'. *Arizona Quarterly* 5 (1963): 357–66.

——. *The Tempering of Eugene O'Neill*. New York: Harcourt, Brace, 1962.

Anderson, Maxwell. *Dramatist in America. Letters of Maxwell Anderson, 1912–1958*. Ed. Lawrence G. Avery. Chapel Hill: The University of North Carolina Press, 1977.

——. *Eleven Verse Plays, 1929–1939*. New York: Harcourt, Brace & Co., 1940. (non-consecutive pagination).

——. *Elizabeth the Queen. Eleven Verse Plays*, 1–131.

——. *'The Essence of Tragedy' and Other Footnotes and Papers*. Washington, D.C.: Anderson House, 1939.

——. 'The Essence of Tragedy'. *'The Essence of Tragedy'*, 1–14.

——. *Joan of Lorraine. Three Plays*, 3–90.

——. *Journey to Jerusalem. Three Plays*, 217–90.

——. *Key Largo. Eleven Verse Plays*, 1–125.

——. *The Masque of Kings. Eleven Verse Plays* 1–139.

——. 'Off Broadway'. *Off Broadway. Essays About the Theatre*, 18–35.

——. *Off Broadway. Essays About the Theatre*. New York: William Sloane Associates, 1947.

——. Preface. *Journey to Jerusalem*, 211–16.

——. 'A Prelude to Poetry in the Theatre'. *'The Essence of Tragedy'* 29–38.

——. *Second Overture. Eleven Verse Plays*, 1–25.

——. *Three Plays by Maxwell Anderson*. New York: Washington Square Press, 1962.

——. 'Whatever Hope We Have'. *'The Essence of Tragedy'*, 15–27.

——. 'Yes, By the Eternal'. *'The Essence of Tragedy'*, 47–53.

Aristotle. *Poetics*. Butcher 6–111.

Asibong, Emmanuel B. *Tennessee Williams: The Tragic Tension*. Stockwell, 1978.

Auden, W. H. 'The Christian Tragic Hero: Contrasting Captain Ahab's Doom and Its Classic Greek Prototype'. *The New York Times Book Review* (16 Dec. 1945): 1, 21. Corrigan, *Tragedy: Vision and Form*, 143–7.

——. 'The Martyr as Dramatic Hero'. *Secondary Worlds*. London, 1968, 15–45.

——. *Secondary Worlds*. (The T.S. Eliot Memorial Lectures) London: Faber and Faber, 1968.

Avery, Laurence G. 'Maxwell Anderson: A Changing Attitude Toward Love'. *Modern Drama* 10 (1967): 241–8.
Bailey, Mabel Driscoll. *Maxwell Anderson: The Playwright as Prophet*. London and New York: Abelard-Schuman, 1957.
Baker, Howard. *Introduction to Tragedy*. Baton Rouge: Louisiana State University Press, 1939.
Bennett, Beate Hein. 'Williams and European Drama: Infernalists and Forgers of Modern Myths'. Tharpe, 429–59.
Bentley, Eric. 'The Innocence of Arthur Miller'. *What is Theatre?*, 62–65.
——. *The Playright as Thinker. A Study of Drama in Modern Times*. 1946. New York: Harcourt, Brace & World, 1967.
——. *The Theatre of Commitment, and Other Essays on Drama in Our Society*. New York: Atheneum, 1967.
——, ed. *The Theory of the Modern Stage: An Introduction to Modern Theatre and Drama*. Harmondsworth: Penguin, 1976.
——. 'Trying to Like O'Neill'. *Kenyon Review* 14 (1952): 476–92. Raleigh, *The Iceman Cometh*, 37–49.
——. *What is Theatre?* New York: Atheneum, 1968.
Berkman, Leonard. 'The Tragic Downfall of Blanche DuBois'. *Modern Drama* 10 (1967): 249–57.
Berlin, Normand. 'Complementarity in *A Streetcar Named Desire*'. Tharpe, 97–103.
——. *Eugene O'Neill*. New York: Grove, 1982.
——. *The Secret Cause: A Discussion of Tragedy*. Boston: University of Massachusetts Press, 1981.
Bhatia, Santosh. *Arthur Miller. Social Drama as Tragedy*. New Delhi: Arnold-Heinemann, 1985.
Bloom, Harold, ed. *Eugene O'Neill's* The Iceman Cometh. New York: Chelsea House, 1987.
——, ed. *Tennessee Williams'* The Glass Menagerie. New York: Chelsea House, 1988.
——, ed. *Tennessee Williams'* A Streetcar Named Desire. New York: Chelsea House, 1988.
——, ed. *Tennessee Williams*. New York: Chelsea House, 1987.
Bigsby, C. W. E. *Confrontation and Commitment. A Study of Contemporary American Drama. 1959–66*. London: MacGibbon & Kee, 1967.
——. *A Critical Introduction to Twentieth-Century American Drama. Volume Two. Williams/Miller/Albee*. Cambridge: Cambridge University Press, 1984.
——. 'The Fall and After: Arthur Miller's Confession'. *Modern Drama* 10 (1967): 137–43. Dorothy Parker, 68–79.
Bock, Hedwig. 'Tennessee Williams, Southern Playwright'. Wertheim and Bock, 5–18.
Bogard, Travis. *Contour in Time. The Plays of Eugene O'Neill*. New York: Oxford University Press, 1972.
Bogard, Travis and William I. Oliver, eds. *Modern Drama. Essays in Criticism*. New York: Oxford University Press, 1965.
Brandt, George. 'Cinematic Structure in the Work of Tennessee Williams'. Brown and Harris, 163–187.

Brashear, William R. 'The Empty Bench: Morality, Tragedy, and Arthur Miller'. *Michigan Quarterly Review* 5 (1966): 270–8.

——. 'The Wisdom of Silenus in O'Neill's *Iceman*'. *American Literature* 36.2 (May 1964): 180–8.

Brooks, Cleanth, ed. *Tragic Themes in Western Literature.* New Haven and London: Yale University Press, 1955.

Brown, John Russell and Bernard Harris, eds. *American Theatre*. Stratford-Upon-Avon Studies 10. London: Edward Arnold, 1967.

Brustein, Robert. *'The Iceman Cometh'*. *The Theatre of Revolt*. Boston and Toronto: Atlantic-Little, Brown and Company, 1965, 336–48. Raleigh, 92–102.

——. 'The Memory of Heroism'. *Tulane Drama Review* 4.3 (March, 1960): 3–9.

Bryer, Jackson R., ed. *'The Theater We Worked For'. The Letters of Eugene O'Neill to Kenneth MacGowan*. New Haven: Yale University Press, 1982.

Butcher, S. H. *Aristotle's Theory of Poetry and Fine Art*. 1895. London: Macmillan, 1923.

Calarco, N. J. *Tragic Being: Apollo and Dionysus in Western Drama.* Minneapolis: University of Minnesota Press, 1969.

Camus, Albert. *La Chute. Recit*. Paris: Gallimard, 1956. *The Fall*. Trans, Justin O'Brien. New York: Knopf, 1978.

——. 'On the Future of Tragedy'. Lecture delivered in Athens, 1955. *Lyrical and Critical Essays*. Trans. Ellen Conroy Kennedy. Ed. Philip Cody. New York: Knopf, 1969, 295–310.

Cardullo, Bert. 'Drama of Intimacy and Tragedy of Incomprehension: *A Streetcar Named Desire* Reconsidered'. Tharpe 137–53.

Cargill, Oscar *et al.*, eds. *O'Neill and His Plays: Four Decades of Criticism.* New York: New York University Press, 1961.

Carpenter, Frederic I. *Eugene O'Neill*. 1964. Boston: Twayne, 1979. Revised.

——. 'Focus on Eugene O'Neill's *The Iceman Cometh*: The Iceman Hath Come'. Madden, 158–64.

——. 'The Romantic Tragedy of Eugene O'Neill'. *College English* 6.5 (Feb. 1945): 250–58.

Carson, Neil. *Arthur Miller*. London: Macmillan, 1982.

Charbrowe, Leonard. *Ritual and Pathos: The Theatre of O'Neill*. Lewisburg, Pa.: Bucknell University Press, 1976.

Clark, Barrett H. *Eugene O'Neill. The Man and His Plays*. 1929. New York: McBride, 1936. Revised.

——. *Maxwell Anderson. The Man and His Plays*. New York: Samuel French, 1933.

Cole, Toby and Helen Krich Chinoy, ed. *Directors on Directing*. New York: Macmillan, 1976.

Cole, Toby, ed. *Playwrights on Playwriting*. New York: Hill and Wang, 1961.

Corrigan, Mary Ann. 'Realism and Theatricalism in *A Streetcar Named Desire*'. *Modern Drama* 19 (Dec. 1976): 385–96. Dorothy Parker 27–38.

Corrigan, Robert W., ed. *Arthur Miller: A Collection of Critical Essays.* Englewood Cliffs: Prentice-Hall, 1969.

——, ed. *Tragedy: Vision and Form*. San Francisco: Chandler, 1965.

Costello, Donald P. 'Tennessee Williams' Fugitive Kind'. *Modern Drama* 15 (May 1972): 26–43.

Davis, Joseph K. 'Landscapes of the Dislocated Mind in Williams' *The Glass Menagerie*'. Tharpe, 192–206.

Day, Cyrus. 'The Iceman and the Bridegroom: Some Observations on the Death of O'Neill's Salesman'. *Modern Drama* 1 (1958): 3–9. Bloom, 9–16.

Debusscher, Gilbert. 'Tennessee Williams' Lives of the Saints: A Playwright's Obliquity'. *Revue des Langues Vivantes* 40.5 (1974): 449–56. Stanton, 149–57.

Devlin, Albert J., ed. *Conversations with Tennessee Williams*. Jackson and London: University Press of Mississippi, 1986.

Downer, Alan S., ed. *American Drama and its Critics. A Collection of Critical Essays*. Toronto: University of Toronto Press, 1965.

——. *The American Theatre Today*. New York: Basic Books, 1967.

——. *Recent American Drama*. Minneapolis: University of Minnesota Press, 1961.

Driver, Tom. *Romantic Quest and Modern Query. A History of the Modern Theatre*. New York: Delacorte, 1970.

——. 'Strength and Weakness in Arthur Miller'. *Tulane Drama Review* 4 (1960): 45–52. Corrigan *Arthur Miller* 59–67.

Dukore, Bernard F. 'The Cat Has Nine Lives'. *Tulane Drama Review* 8 (Fall 1973): 95–100.

Durham, Frank. 'Tennessee Williams, Theatre Poet in Prose'. *South Atlantic Bulletin* 36 (1971): 3–16. Parker, *The Glass Menagerie*, 121–34.

Dusenburg, Winifred L. *The Theme of Loneliness in Modern American Drama*. Gainesville: University of Florida Press, 1960, 1967.

Ehrlich, Alan. 'A Streetcar Named Desire Under the Elms: A Study of Dramatic Space in *A Streetcar Named Desire*'. Tharpe 126–36.

Eliot, T.S. 'Tradition and the Individual Talent'. *Selected Essays 1917–1932*, London: Faber & Faber, 1932.

Engel, Edwin. *The Haunted Heroes of Eugene O'Neill*. Cambridge: Harvard University Press, 1953.

Evans, Richard I. *Psychology and Arthur Miller*. New York: Dutton, 1969.

Faas, Ekbert. *Tragedy and After. Euripides, Shakespeare, Goethe*. Kingston and Montreal: McGill-Queen's University Press, 1984.

Falk, Doris V. *Eugene O'Neill and the Tragic Tension*. New Brunswick, N.J.: Rutgers University Press, 1958.

——. 'That Paradox, Eugene O'Neill'. *Modern Drama* 6 (1963): 221–38.

Falk, Signi. *Tennessee Williams*. 1961. Boston: Twayne Publishers, 1978. Revised.

Fergusson, Francis. *The Idea of a Theater. A Study of Ten Plays. The Art of Drama in Changing Perspective*. 1949. Princeton: Princeton University Press, 1972.

Ferres, John H., ed. *The Crucible. A Collection of Critical Essays*. Englewood Cliffs: Prentice-Hall, 1972.

Floyd, Virginia, ed. *Eugene O'Neill at Work: Newly Released Ideas for Plays*. New York: Ungar, 1981.

——, ed. *Eugene O'Neill: A World View*. New York: Ungar, 1979.
——. *The Plays of Eugene O'Neill. A New Assessment*. New York: Ungar, 1985.
Foster, Edward. 'Core of Belief'. *Sewanee Review* 50 (1942): 87–100.
Foster, John Burt, Jr. *Heirs to Dionysus. A Nietzschean Current in Literary Modernism*. Princeton: Princeton University Press, 1981.
Frazer, Winifred. 'King Lear and Hickey: Bridegroom and Iceman'. *Modern Drama* 15 (1973): 267–78.
——. 'Revolution in *The Iceman Cometh*'. *Modern Drama* 22 (1979): 1–8.
Frenz, Horst, ed. *American Playwrights on Drama*. New York: Hill and Wang, 1965.
Frye, Northrop. *Anatomy of Criticism: Four Essays*. Princeton: Princeton University Press, 1957.
Ganz, Arthur. 'Arthur Miller: After the Silence'. *Drama Survey* 3 (1964): 520–30.
——. 'The Desperate Morality of the Plays of Tennessee Williams'. *American Scholar* 31 (Spring 1962): 278–94.
Downer, *American Drama and its Critics* 203–17. Stanton 123–37.
——. 'The Silence of Arthur Miller'. *Drama Survey* 3 (Oct. 1963): 224–37.
Gassner, John T. *Directions in Modern Theatre and Drama*. New York: Holt, Rinehart and Winston, 1965.
——. *Dramatic Soundings. Evaluations and Refractions Culled from 30 Years of Dramatic Criticism*. New York: Crown, 1968.
——. *Eugene O'Neill*. Minneapolis: University of Minnesota Press, 1965.
——. 'Heroism and the American Theatre'. *Tomorrow* (May 1943). *Dramatic Soundings*.
——. *Ideas in the Drama. Selected Papers from the English Institute*. New York: Columbia University Press, 1964.
——, ed. *O'Neill. A Collection of Critical Essays*. Englewood Cliffs: Prentice-Hall, 1964.
——. 'The Possibilities and Perils of Modern Tragedy'. *Tulane Drama Review* 1.3 (June 1957): 3–14. Corrigan, *Tragedy: Vision and Form*, 405–17.
——. '*A Streetcar Named Desire*: A Study in Ambiguity'. *The Theatre in Our Times*, 355–363. Bogard and Oliver, 374–84.
——. 'Tennessee Williams: Dramatist of Frustration'. *College English* 10 (Oct. 1948): 1–7.
——. *The Theatre in Our Times. A Survey of the Men, Materials and Movements in the Modern Theatre*. New York: Crown, 1954.
——. 'Tragedy in the Modern Theatre'. *The Theatre in Our Times*, 51–74.
——. 'Tragic Perspectives: A Sequence of Queries'. *Tulane Drama Review* 2 (May 1958): 7–22.
Gelb, Arthur and Barbara Gelb, eds. *O'Neill*. 1962. New York: Harper, 1973. Revised.
Glicksberg, Charles I. *The Self in Modern Literature*. University Park, Pennsylvania: The Pennsylvania State University Press, 1963.
——. *The Tragic Vision in Twentieth-Century Literature*. Carbondale, Ill.: Southern Illinois University Press, 1963.
Golden, Joseph. *The Death of Tinker Bell; the American Theatre in the 20th Century*. Syracuse: Syracuse University Press, 1967.

Griffin, Ernest G., ed. *Eugene O'Neill: A Collection of Criticism*. New York: McGraw Hill, 1976.

Grimm, Reinhold. 'A Note on O'Neill, Nietzsche, and Naturalism: *Long Day's Journey into Night* in European Perspective'. *Modern Drama* 26 (Sept. 1983): 331–4.

Groff, Edward. 'Point of View in Modern Drama'. *Modern Drama* 2 (1959): 268–82.

Gross, Barry. '*All My Sons* and the Larger Context'. *Modern Drama* 18 (1975): 15–27. Dorothy Parker, 55–67.

Halline, Allan G. 'Maxwell Anderson's Dramatic Theory'. *American Literature* 16 (1944): 63–81.

Harris, Mark. *The Case for Tragedy*. New York: Putnam's, 1932.

Harwood, Britton J. 'Tragedy as Habit: *A Streetcar Named Desire*'. Tharpe, 104–15.

Hauser, Arnold. 'The Origins of Domestic Drama'. *Social History of Art*. 1952. Trans. Stanley Goodman and Arnold Hauser. Bentley, *The Theory of the Modern Stage* 403–19.

——. *The Social History of Art*. Vol. 4 Trans. Stanley Godman. New York: Random House, n.d.

Hayman, Ronald. 'Arthur Miller: Between Sartre and Society'. *Encounter* 37 (Nov. 1971): 73–79.

——. *Arthur Miller*. London: Heinemann, 1970.

Hegel, G. W. 'Tragedy as a Dramatic Art' and 'Dramatic Action and Character'. *The Theory of Fine Art* vols. i and iv. *On Tragedy*. Ed. Anne Paolucci and Henry Paolucci. New York: Harper and Row, 1962.

Heilman, Robert B. *The Iceman, The Arsonist, and the Troubled Agent. Tragedy and Melodrama on the Modern Stage*. Seattle: University of Washington Press, 1973.

——. 'Tennessee Williams: Approach to Tragedy'. *Southern Review* 1 (Autumn 1965): 770–90.

——. *Tragedy and Melodrama: Versions of Experience*. Seattle: University of Washington Press, 1968.

Henn, T. R. *The Harvest of Tragedy*. London: Methuen, 1956.

Hogan, Robert. *Arthur Miller*. Minneapolis: University of Minnesota Press, 1964.

Huftel, Sheila. *Arthur Miller: The Burning Glass*. New York: Citadel, 1965.

Hurrell, John D. ed. *Two Modern American Tragedies. Reviews and Criticism of 'Death of a Salesman' and 'A Streetcar Named Desire'*. New York: Charles Scribner's Sons, 1961.

Huxley, Aldous. 'Tragedy and the Whole Truth'. *Collected Essays*. London: Harper and Row, 1959, 96–103. Corrigan, *Tragedy: Vision and Form* 76–82.

Jackson, Esther Merle. *The Broken World of Tennessee Williams*. Madison: University of Wisconsin Press, 1965.

——. 'Tennessee Williams: Poetic Consciousness in Crisis'. Tharpe, 53–72.

Jones, Robert Emmet. 'Tennessee Williams' Early Heroines'. *Modern Drama* 2 (1959): 211–19.

Joyce, James. *A Portrait of the Artist as a Young Man*. 1916, London: Penguin, 1976.

Kahn, Sy. 'Through a Glass Menagerie Darkly: The World of Tennessee Williams'. Taylor, 71–90.
Kaufmann, Walter. *Tragedy and Philosophy*. Princeton: Princeton University Press, 1979.
Kazan, Elia. 'A Notebook for *A Streetcar Named Desire*'. Cole and Chinoy 364–79.
Kazin, Alfred. *On Native Grounds*. New York: Harcourt Brace Jovanovich, 1942.
Kierkegaard, Soren. 'The Ancient Tragical Motif as Reflected in the Modern'. *Either/Or; A Fragment of Life*, Vol. 1., 1843. Trans. David Swenson and Lillian M. Swenson. Princeton: Princeton University Press, 1944, 111–33. Corrigan, *Tragedy: Vision and Form*, 451–70.
King, Thomas L. 'Irony and Distance in *The Glass Menagerie*'. *Educational Theatre Journal* 25 (May 1973): 207–14. Parker, *The Glass Menagerie*, 75–86.
Krieger, Murray. *The Tragic Vision. Variations on a Theme in Literary Interpretation*. Chicago: Chicago University Press, 1966.
Krook, Dorothea. *Elements of Tragedy*. New Haven and London: Yale University Press, 1969.
Krutch, Joseph Wood. *The American Drama since 1918. An Informal History*. New York: Random House, 1939.
——. Introduction. O'Neill, *Nine Plays*, xi–xxii.
——. *The Modern Temper. A Study and a Confession*. New York: Harcourt, Brace and Company, 1929.
——. *'Modernism' in Modern Drama. A Definition and an Estimate*. Ithaca: Cornell University Press, 1953.
——. 'O'Neill's Tragic Sense'. *American Scholar* 16 (Summer 1947): 285.
Langer, Susanne. 'The Tragic Rhythm'. *Feeling and Form*. New York: Charles Scribner's Sons, 1953. Corrigan, *Tragedy*, 85–98.
Leech, Clifford. *Eugene O'Neill*. New York: Grove Press, 1963.
Lillo, George. *The London Merchant*. Lincoln: University of Nebraska Press, 1965.
Londré, Felicia Hardison. *Tennessee Williams*. New York: Ungar, 1979.
——. *Tennessee Williams: Life, Work, and Criticism*. Fredericton: York Press, 1989.
Lucas, F. L. *Tragedy in Relation to Aristotle's Poetics*. London: Hogarth Press, 1928.
Lukács, George. 'The Sociology of Modern Drama'. 1909 (Hungarian original). 1914 (German version. *Archiv für Sozialwissenschaft und Sozialpolitik*.) Trans. Lee Baxandall. *Tulane Drama Review* 9.4 (Summer, 1965): 146–70. Bentley, *The Theory of the Modern Stage*, 425–50.
MacGowan, Kenneth. *The Theatre of Tomorrow*. London: Unwin, 1923.
Madden, David ed. *American Dreams, American Nightmares*. Carbondale and Edwardsville: Southern Illinois University Press.
Maeterlinck, Maurice. 'The Tragical in Daily Life'. *The Treasure of the Humble*. Trans. Alfred Sutro. New York: Dodd, Mead and Co., 1916, 103–19. Cole, *Playwrights on Playwriting*, 30–6.
Manheim, Michael. *Eugene O'Neill's New Language of Kinship*. Syracuse: Syracuse University Press, 1982.

Martin, Robert A. 'Arthur Miller's *The Crucible*: Background and Sources'. *Modern Drama* 20 (1977): 279–92. Dorothy Parker, 80–93.

——, ed. *Arthur Miller. (New Perspectives)* Englewood Cliffs, N.J.: Prentice-Hall, 1982.

Martine, James J., ed. *Critical Essays on Eugene O'Neill*. Boston: G.K. Hall & Co., 1984.

Martz, Louis L. 'The Saint as Tragic Hero. *Saint Joan* and *Murder in the Cathedral*'. Brooks, 150–78.

May, Charles E. 'Brick Pollitt as Homo Ludens: 'Three Players of a Summer Game' and *Cat on a Hot Tin Roof*'. Tharpe, 277–91.

McAnany, Emile G. 'The Tragic Commitment: Some Notes on Arthur Miller'. *Modern Drama* 5 (1962): 11–20.

Michel, Laurence and Richard B. Sewall, eds. *Tragedy: Modern Essays in Criticism*. Englewood Cliffs: Prentice-Hall, 1963.

Miller, Arthur. *After the Fall. Collected Plays* Vol. 2, 125–242.

——. *All My Sons. Collected Plays* Vol. 1, 58–127.

——. *Arthur Miller's Collected Plays* Vol. 1 New York: Viking, 1957.

——. *Arthur Miller's Collected Plays* Vol. 2 New York: Viking, 1981.

——. 'Brewed in *The Crucible*'. *The New York Times* (9 March 1958): sec 2. 3. *The Theater Essays*, 171–4.

——. *The Crucible. Collected Plays* Vol. 1, 225–329.

——. *Death of a Salesman. Collected Plays* Vol. 1, 130–222.

——. 'The Family in Modern Drama'. *The Atlantic Monthly* 197 (April 1956): 35–41. *The Theater Essays*, 69–85.

——. 'Foreword to *After the Fall*'. *The Saturday Evening Post* 237 (1 Feb. 1964): 32. *The Theater Essays*, 255–7.

——. Interview. 'Arthur Miller and the Meaning of Tragedy'. With Robert A. Martin. *Modern Drama* 13 (1970): 34–9.

——. Interview. 'Morality and Modern Drama'. With Philip Gelb. *Educational Theatre Journal* 10 (Oct. 1958): 190–202. *The Theater Essays*, 195–214.

——. Interview. 'The State of the Theater'. With Henry Brandon. *Harper's* 221 (Nov. 1960): 63–9. *The Theater Essays*, 223–36.

——. Interview. ''The Will to Live'. An Interview with Arthur Miller'. With Steven R. Centola. *Modern Drama* 27 (1984): 345–60.

——. 'Introduction to the Collected Plays'. *Collected Plays* Vol. 1, 3–55.

——. 'The Nature of Tragedy'. *New York Herald Tribune* (27 March 1949): sec. 5, 1–2. *The Theater Essays*, 8–11.

——. 'On Social Plays'. Preface. *A View from the Bridge*. One-act version. New York: Viking, 1955, 1–18. *The Theater Essays*, 51–68.

——. 'The Shadows of the Gods'. *Harper's* 217(Aug. 1958): 35–43. *The Theater Essays*, 175–94.

——. *Timebends. A Life*. New York: Grove, 1987.

——. *The Theater Essays of Arthur Miller*. Ed. Robert A. Martin. New York: Viking, 1978.

——. 'Tragedy and the Common Man'. *New York Times* (27 Feb. 1949): sec 2. 1, 3. *The Theater Essays*, 3–7.

Miller, Jordan Y., ed. *A Streetcar Named Desire. A Collection of Critical Essays*. Englewood Cliffs: Prentice-Hall, 1971.

Mordden, Ethan. *The American Theatre*. New York: Oxford University Press, 1981.
Moss, Leonard. *Arthur Miller*. New York: Twayne, 1967.
——. 'Arthur Miller and the Common Man's Language'. *Modern Drama* 7 (1964): 52–9.
Mottram, Eric. 'Arthur Miller: The Development of a Political Dramatist in America'. *American Theatre*, 127–162. Corrigan, *Arthur Miller*, 23–57.
Muller, Herbert J. *The Spirit of Tragedy*. New York: Knopf, 1956.
Murray, Edward. *Arthur Miller, Dramatist*. New York: Ungar, 1967.
Nathan, George Jean. *The Intimate Notebooks of George Jean Nathan*. New York: Knopf, 1932.
——. *The Magic Mirror. Selected Writings on the Theatre*. New York: Knopf, 1960.
Nelson, Benjamin. *Arthur Miller. Portrait of a Playwright*. New York: McKay, 1970.
——. *Tennessee Williams: The Man and His Work*. New York: Obolensky, 1961.
Niesen, George. 'The Artist against Reality in the Plays of Tennessee Williams'. Tharpe, 463–93.
Nietzsche, Friedrich. *The Birth of Tragedy*. 1872. The Birth of Tragedy *and* The Genealogy of Morals. Trans. F. Golffing. Garden City: Doubleday, 1956.
——. *Thus Spake Zarathustra*. 1883. Trans. R. J. Hollindale. Harmondsworth: Penguin, 1969.
Nolan, Paul T. 'Two Memory Plays: *The Glass Menagerie* and *After the Fall*'. *The McNeese Review* 17 (1966): 27–38. Parker, *The Glass Menagerie* .
Olson, Elder. *Tragedy and the Theory of Drama*. Detroit: Wayne State University Press, 1961.
O'Neill, Eugene. 'Damn the Optimists!' *New York Tribune* (13 Feb. 1921) Cargill, 104–6.
——. Interview. 'The Extraordinary Story of Eugene O'Neill'. With Mary Mullett. *American Magazine* 94 (Nov. 1922): 118, 120. Törnqvist, *A Drama of Souls*, 14.
——. Interview. *New York Herald Tribune* (16 March 1924). Cargill, 110–12.
——. Interview. 'What the Theatre Means to Me'. With Oliver M. Sayler. *Century Magazine* (Jan. 1922) Cargill, 107.
——. *The Iceman Cometh*. New York: Random House, 1946.
——. Letter to Arthur Hobson Quinn. Quinn 199.
——. *Long Day's Journey into Night*. New Haven: Yale University Press, 1956.
——. 'Memoranda on Masks'. *The American Spectator*. Nov., Dec. 1923, Jan. 1933. Cargill, 116–22.
——. *Nine Plays*. New York: Modern Library, 1952.
——. Playbill for *The Spook Sonata*. 'Strindberg and our Theatre'. Jan. 3, 1924. Cargill, 108–9.
——. *'The Theater We Worked For'. The Letters of Eugene O'Neill to Kenneth MacGowan*. Ed. Jackson R. Bryer. New Haven: Yale University Press, 1982.
Orr, John. *Tragic Drama and Modern Society. Studies in the Social and*

Literary Theory of Drama from 1870 to the Present. London: Macmillan, 1981.

Overland, Orm. 'The Action and Its Significance: Arthur Miller's Struggle with Dramatic Form'. *Modern Drama* 18 (1975): 1–14.

Paolucci, Anne and Henry Paolucci, eds. *Hegel on Tragedy*. New York: Harper & Row, 1962.

Parker, R. Brian. 'The Circle Closed: A Psychological Reading of *The Glass Menagerie* and *The Two Character Play*'. *Modern Drama* 28 (1985). Bloom, *The Glass Menagerie* 119–36.

——. 'The Composition of *The Glass Menagerie*. An Argument for Complexity'. *Modern Drama* 25 (1982): 409–22. Dorothy Parker, 12–26.

——, ed. *The Glass Menagerie. A Collection of Critical Essays*. Englewood Cliffs: Prentice-Hall, 1983.

——. 'Point of View in Arthur Miller's *Death of a Salesman*'. *University of Toronto Quarterly* 35 (1966): 144–57. Corrigan, *Arthur Miller*, 95–109.

Parker, Dorothy, ed. *Essays on Modern American Drama. Williams, Miller, Albee and Shepard*. Toronto: University of Toronto Press, 1987.

Porter, Thomas E. *Myth and Modern American Drama*. Detroit: Wayne State University Press, 1969.

Quinn, Arthur Hobson. *A History of the American Drama from the Civil War to the Present Day* Vol. 2. New York and London: Harper & Brothers, 1927.

Rabkin, Gerald. *Drama and Commitment. Politics in the American Theatre of the Thirties*. Bloomington: Indiana University Press, 1964.

——. 'The Political Paradox of Maxwell Anderson'. *Drama and Commitment*, 263–91.

Raleigh, John Henry, ed. *The Iceman Cometh. A Collection of Critical Essays*. Englewood Cliffs: Prentice-Hall, 1968.

——. 'The Last Confession: O'Neill and the Catholic Confessional'. Floyd, *Eugene O'Neill: A World View*, 212–28.

——. *The Plays of Eugene O'Neill*. Carbondale: Southern Illinois University Press, 1965.

Ranald, Margaret Loftus. *The Eugene O'Neill Companion*. Westport: Greenwood Press, 1984.

Riddel, Joseph N. '*A Streetcar Named Desire*. Nietzsche Descending'. *Modern Drama* 5 (Winter 1963): 421–30.

Riepe, Dale. 'The Philosophy of Maxwell Anderson'. *North Dakota Quarterly* 24.2 (1956):.

Robey, Cora. 'Chloroses – Pâles Roses and Pleurosis – Blue Roses'. *Romance Notes* 13 (1971): 250–1.

Rodell, J. S. 'Maxwell Anderson: A Criticism'. *Kenyon Review* 5 (1943): 272–7.

Ross, Don. 'Williams in Art and Morals: An Anxious Foe of Untruth'. Interview. *New York Herald Tribune* (3 March 1957). Devlin, 42.

Sampley, Arthur M. 'Theory and Practice in Maxwell Anderson's Poetic Tragedies'. *College English* 5 (1944): 412–18.

Sartre, Jean-Paul. 'Forgers of Myths. The Young Playwrights of France'. Trans. Rosamond Gilder. *Theatre Arts* 30.6 (June 1946): 324–35.

Schlueter, June and James K Flanagan. *Arthur Miller*. New York: Ungar, 1987.

Schopenhauer, Arthur. *The World as Will and Idea.* Trans. R. B. Haldane and J. Kemp. London: Trubner, 1803.

Shaeffer, Louis. *O'Neill: Son and Playwright*. Boston: Little, Brown, 1968.

——. *O'Neill: Son and Artist*. Boston: Little, Brown, 1974.

Sewall, Richard B. *The Vision of Tragedy*. New Haven: Yale University Press, 1959.

Shaw, George Bernard. *Saint Joan. Complete Plays with Prefaces.* New York: Dodd, Mead & Co., 1962.

Shivers, Alfred S. *The Life of Maxwell Anderson*. New York: Stein and Day, 1983.

——. *Maxwell Anderson*. Bloomington, Indiana: Twayne, 1976.

Siegel, Paul N. 'Willy Loman and King Lear'. *College English* 17 (1956): 341–5.

Stanton, Stephen S. ed. *Tennessee Williams. A Collection of Critical Essays.* Englewood Cliffs: Prentice-Hall, 1977.

Steinberg, M. W. 'Arthur Miller and the Idea of Modern Tragedy'. *Dalhousie Review* 40 (1960): 329–40. Corrigan, *Arthur Miller*, 81–93.

Steiner, George. *The Death of Tragedy*. New York: Knopf, 1961.

Styan, J. L. *The Dark Comedy: The Development of Modern Comic Tragedy.* Cambridge: Cambridge University Press, 1962.

Taylor, William E. 'Maxwell Anderson: Traditionalist in a Theatre of Change'. *Modern American Drama: Essays in Criticism*, 47–57.

——. *Modern American Drama: Essays in Criticism*. DeLand, Fla.: Everett/Edwards, 1968.

Tharpe, Jac, ed. *Tennessee Williams: A Tribute.* Jackson: University Press of Mississippi, 1977.

Thompson, Judith. *Tennessee Williams's Plays: Memory, Myth and Symbol.* New York: Peter Lang, 1987.

Tischler, Nancy. *Tennessee Williams: Rebellious Puritan*. New York: Citadel, 1961.

Tiusanen, Timo. *O'Neill's Scenic Images.* Princeton: Princeton University Press, 1968.

Törnqvist, Egil. *A Drama of Souls. Studies in O'Neill's Supernaturalistic Technique*. New Haven and London: Yale University Press, 1969.

——. '*Miss Julie* and O'Neill'. *Modern Drama* 19 (1976): 351–64.

——. 'Personal Nomenclature in the Plays of O'Neill'. *Modern Drama* 8 (1966): 362–73.

Traubitz, Nancy Baker. 'Myth as a Basis of Dramatic Structure in *Orpheus Descending*'. *Modern Drama* 19 (1976): 57–66. Dorothy Parker 3–11.

Trowbridge, Clinton W. 'Arthur Miller: Between Pathos and Tragedy'. *Modern Drama* 10 (1967): 221–32.

Unamuno, Miguel de. *Tragic Sense of Life*. 1913. Trans. J. B. Crawford Flitch. London: Macmillan, 1926.

Valgemae, Mardi. *Accelerated Grimace. Expressionism in the American Drama of the 1920s*. Carbondale: Southern Illinois University Press, 1972.

——. 'O'Neill and German Expressionism'. *Modern Drama* 10 (1967): 111–23.

Vogel, Dan. *The Three Masks of American Tragedy*. Baton Rouge: Louisiana State University Press, 1974.

Von Szeliski, John. *Tragedy and Fear. Why Modern Tragic Drama Fails*. Chapel Hill: University of North Carolina Press, 1962, 1971.

Vowles, Richard B. 'Tennessee Williams and Strindberg'. *Modern Drama* 1 (Dec. 1958): 166–71.

Wall, Vincent. 'Maxwell Anderson: The Last Anarchist'. *The Sewanee Review* 49 (1941): 340–69.

Warshow, Robert. 'The Gangster as Tragic Hero'. *Partisan Review* 15.2 (Feb. 1948): 240–4. Corrigan, *Tragedy: Vision and Form*, 152–6.

——. 'The Liberal Conscience in *The Crucible*'. *Commentary* 15 (March 1953): 265–71. *The Immediate Experience*. New York: Doubleday, 1962. Corrigan, *Arthur Miller*, 111–21.

Watts, Harold H. 'Maxwell Anderson: The Tragedy of Attrition'. *College English* 4 (1943): 220–30.

Weales, Gerald. *American Drama Since World War II*. New York: Harcourt, Brace & World, 1962.

——, ed. *Arthur Miller: Death of a Salesman*. New York: Viking, 1967.

——. 'Arthur Miller: Man and His Image'. *The Drama Review* 7.1 (Fall 1962): 165–80.

——, ed. *Arthur Miller: The Crucible*. New York: Viking, 1971.

——. 'Arthur Miller's Shifting Image of Man'. Corrigan, *Arthur Miller*, 131–42.

——. *The Jumping-Off Place. American Drama in the 1960's*. New York: Macmillan, 1969.

——. *Tennessee Williams*. Minneapolis: University of Minnesota Press, 1965.

Weisinger, Herbert. *Tragedy and the Paradox of the Fortunate Fall*. East Lansing: Michigan State College Press, 1953.

Welch, Dennis M. 'Hickey as Satanic Force in *The Iceman Cometh*'. *Arizona Quarterly* 34 (1978): 219–29.

Welland, Dennis. *Arthur Miller*. Edinburgh: Oliver & Boyd, 1961.

——. *Miller: A Study of his Plays*. London: Methuen, 1979.

Wertheim, Albert and Hedwick Bock, eds. *Essays on Contemporary American Drama*. Munich: Hueber, 1981.

Wertheim, Albert. 'Arthur Miller: After the Fall and After'. Wertheim and Bock, 19–32.

Wickhamkoon, Helen. ed. *Death of a Salesman. A Collection of Critical Essays*. Englewood Cliffs: Prentice-Hall, 1983.

Willett, Ralph W. 'The Ideas of Miller and Williams'. *Theatre Annual* 22 (1966): 31–40.

Williams, Raymond. *Drama from Ibsen to Brecht*. Harmondsworth: Penguin, 1976.

——. *Modern Tragedy*. 1966. London: Verso Edition, 1979. Revised.

——. 'The Realism of Arthur Miller'. *Critical Quarterly* 1 (Summer 1959): 140–9. Corrigan, *Arthur Miller* 69–79.

Williams, Tennessee. *Cat on a Hot Tin Roof*. New York: Signet, 1955.

——. 'The Catastrophe of Success'. Introduction. *The Glass Menagerie* 11–17.

——. *The Glass Menagerie*. New York: New Directions, 1966.
——. Interviews. *Conversations with Tennessee Williams*. Ed. Albert J. Devlin. Jackson and London: University Press of Mississippi, 1986.
——. 'Interview with Tennessee Williams'. With Cecil Brown. *Partisan Review*, 45 (1978): 276–305. Devlin, 251–83.
——. Interview. 'Williams in Art and Morals: An Anxious Foe of Untruth'. With Don Ross. *New York Herald Tribune* (3 March 1957). Devlin, 38–53.
——. *Memoirs*. Garden City, New York: Doubleday, 1975.
——. 'Note of Explanation'. *Cat on a Hot Tin Roof*, 124–25.
——. 'On a Streetcar Named Success'. *Where I Live*.
——. *Orpheus Descending*. Orpheus Descending *with* Battle of Angels. *Two Plays by Tennessee Williams*. New York: New Directions, 1958, 2–118.
——. 'The Past, the Present and the Perhaps'. *New York Times* (17 March 1957). Preface. *Orpheus Descending*, v–x.
——. 'Person-to-Person'. *Cat on a Hot Tin Roof*, vii–x.
——. 'Production Notes'. *The Glass Menagerie*, 7–10.
——. 'Questions Without Answers'. *Where I Live*.
——. *A Streetcar Named Desire*. New York: New Directions, 1947.
——. 'Tennessee Williams Presents his P.O.V'. *Where I Live*.
——. *Tennessee Williams' Letters to Donald Windham 1940–1965*. ed. Donald Windham. New York: Holt, Rinehart, and Winston, 1976.
——. 'The Timeless World of the Play'. Introduction. *The Rose Tattoo* (1951). *Where I Live*.
——. *Where I Live. Selected Essays*. New York: New Directions, 1978.
Winther, Sophus Keith. *Eugene O'Neill: A Critical Study*. 1934. New York: Russell & Russell, 1961.
——. 'O'Neill's Tragic Themes: *Long Day's Journey into Night*'. *Arizona Quarterly* 13 (1957): 295–307.
Wright, Robert C. 'O'Neill's Universalizing Technique in *The Iceman Cometh*'. *Modern Drama* 8 (1965): 1–11.
Young, Vernon. 'Social Drama and Big Daddy'. *Southwest Review* 41 (Spring 1956): 194–7.

Index

continued overleaf